Cracking MATHS
5th Class Pupil's Book

Brian O'Doherty

GILL EDUCATION

Gill Education
Hume Avenue
Park West
Dublin 12
www.gilleducation.ie
Gill Education is an imprint of M.H. Gill & Co.

ISBN: 978 07171 53879

Design: Design Image and Richard Jervis
Internal illustrations: Kate Shannon
Technical drawings: Design Image
Cover illustration: www.designbos.ie
Consultant editor in mathematics curriculum and pedagogy: Betty Stoutt
Mathematics consultant: Oliver Hyde

The paper used in this book comes from the wood pulp of managed forests. For every tree felled, at least one tree is planted, thereby renewing natural resources.

Any links to external websites should not be construed as an endorsement by Gill & Macmillan of the content or view of the linked material.

All photos © Shutterstock

The publishers have made every effort to contact copyright holders but any omissions will be rectified at the next reprint.

The author would like to acknowledge the significant contribution made by Aoife Travers in the development of these materials.

Contents

1. Look Back

Summer Sun

Polly Brown and her twin sister, Holly, went on holidays with their parents to Italy during the summer. The cost of a ticket for an adult was €345 and the cost of a ticket for a child was €187.

The flight was due to take off at 1:15pm but they were told to check in 2 hours before take-off time.

They brought 3 suitcases with them. The 1st suitcase was checked in and weighed 38kg. The 2nd suitcase weighed 29kg and the 3rd suitcase weighed 33kg.

When their passports had been checked they went through to the boarding area and onto the plane. The plane was an Airbus 320 and had 27 rows of 6 seats, 3 on either side of the aisle. The plane took off exactly on time and the flight lasted 1 hour 55 minutes.

After they landed in Rome and got their suitcases, Mr Brown rented a car for a week. The cost of the car was €45 per day.

During the course of the week they made the following journeys.

Rome to Florence: 326km   Turin to Verona: 276km
Florence to Turin: 193km   Verona to Rome: 309km

When they were in Verona the family did a little shopping. Polly had €40 and she spent $\frac{1}{2}$ of it on a CD, $\frac{1}{4}$ of it on a new purse and $\frac{1}{8}$ of it on a souvenir. The souvenir she bought was a cube that had photographs of a different tourist attraction on each side.

All in all, the family had a wonderful holiday and they hope to go somewhere else next year.

1. How much did the 2 adult tickets cost in total?

2. How much did the 2 children's tickets cost in total?

3. What was the difference in price between an adult's ticket and a child's ticket?

Curriculum Objectives:
To revise concepts that were explored in 4th class.

4. What was the total cost of the family's tickets?

5. If Polly was an only child, what would the total cost of the family's tickets be?

6. At what time should the family have checked in at the airport?

7. They boarded the plane 20 minutes before take-off time. What time was that?

8. At what time did they land in Rome?

9. If it took another 35 minutes after they landed to go through passport control and get their luggage, at what time did they leave the airport in Rome?

10. How many seats were on the plane altogether?

11. If 19 of the seats were unoccupied, how many people were on the flight altogether?

12. The day before there had been 3 flights to Rome and each of them was full. How many people travelled?

13. How much did it cost the family to hire the car for the week?

14. If there was a special offer and the car hire company gave the family a discount of €6 a day, how much would it cost to hire the car?

15. What was the total distance travelled in the car?

16. How much longer was the journey from Rome to Florence than the journey from Florence to Turin?

17. If the family had taken the wrong road on the way to Verona and driven an extra 48km, what distance would they have travelled that day?

18. If you drove from Verona to Florence through Turin, what distance would you have driven?

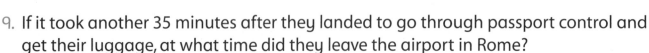

19. How much did Polly's CD cost?

20. How much did Polly's new purse cost?

21. How much did Polly's souvenir cost?

22. What change had she from her €40 after buying the 3 items?

23. How many different photographs were on the souvenir cube?

24. If it had been a souvenir pyramid, how many different photographs would there have been?

1. Complete these mathematical sentences.
   a) $135 + 1983 + 538 =$
   b) $2156 + 3548 =$
   c) $5198 + 46 + 924 =$
   d) $673 + 1884 + 2190 =$
   e) $164 - 87 =$
   f) $2035 - 1462 =$
   g) $8833 - 3497 =$
   h) $5412 - 1979 =$
   i) $238 \times 7 =$
   j) $419 \times 6 =$
   k) $125 \times 9 =$
   l) $643 \times 8 =$
   m) $43 \times 25 =$
   n) $59 \times 18 =$
   o) $138 \times 27 =$
   p) $246 \times 34 =$
   q) $243 \div 9 =$
   r) $568 \div 8 =$
   s) $1596 \div 7 =$
   t) $3576 \div 6 =$
   u) $1988 \div 4 =$

2. Write the next 3 terms of each of these sequences.
   a) 91, 93, 95, 97, ____, ____, ____
   b) 680, 685, 690, 695, ____, ____, ____
   c) 1008, 1006, 1004, 1002, ____, ____, ____
   d) 1712, 1812, 1912, ____, ____, ____

3. a) What is $\frac{1}{2}$ of 42?
   b) What is $\frac{1}{3}$ of 90?
   c) What is $\frac{1}{4}$ of 56?
   d) What is $\frac{3}{4}$ of 36?
   e) What is $\frac{2}{5}$ of 45?
   f) What is $\frac{5}{6}$ of 54?
   g) What is $\frac{5}{8}$ of 40?
   h) What is $\frac{9}{10}$ of 90?

4. a) $\frac{1}{4}$ of a number is 20. What is the number?
   b) $\frac{1}{3}$ of a number is 27. What is the number?
   c) $\frac{1}{6}$ of a number is 15. What is the number?
   d) $\frac{4}{5}$ of a number is 16. What is the number?
   e) $\frac{5}{9}$ of a number is 45. What is the number?
   f) $\frac{7}{8}$ of a number is 42. What is the number?

5. a) How many minutes are there in 1 hour 13 minutes?
   b) How many minutes are there in 1 hour 47 minutes?
   c) How many minutes are there in 1 hour 58 minutes?
   d) How many minutes are there in 2 hours 26 minutes?
   e) How many minutes are there in 3 hours 34 minutes?
   f) How many minutes are there in 5 hours?

6. a) How many hours and minutes are there in 93 minutes?
   b) How many hours and minutes are there in 116 minutes?
   c) How many hours and minutes are there in 125 minutes?
   d) How many hours and minutes are there in 149 minutes?
   e) How many hours and minutes are there in 198 minutes?
   f) How many hours and minutes are there in 275 minutes?

2. Place Value

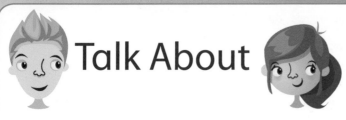

Talk About

Roman Numerals

Here is a number system that the Romans used many years ago.

$$I – 1$$
$$V – 5$$
$$X – 10$$
$$L – 50$$
$$C – 100$$
$$D – 500$$
$$M – 1000$$

The Romans had different symbols for some of their numbers and formed other numbers by combining these symbols.

For example, 236 written in Roman numerals would be CCXXXVI.

1. Have a go at writing these numbers as Roman numerals.

   a) 7   b) 15   c) 9   d) 11   e) 23
   f) 35   g) 27   h) 49   i) 52   j) 98
   k) 136   l) 167   m) 913   n) 1250   o) 4999

Have at look at this simple addition sum using Roman numerals:

CCXXXVI + CCXXXVI = CCCCXXXXXXVVII (236 + 236 =)

We can now try to reduce the amount of symbols by renaming some of them:

XXXXXX = 60 = LX and VV = 10 = X

So the answer now reads CCCCLXXII (or 472 to you and me!).

Strand: Number
Curriculum Objectives:
Read, write and order whole numbers and decimals;
identify place value in whole numbers and decimals;
round whole numbers and round decimals.

2. Try these if you dare!
   a) CCLXXVI + CXXXIII
   b) DCXXVI + DCCCXV
   c) CLXXVI × V (Remember: V × I, or 5 × I, is still 5 no matter what the number system is.)
   d) XXXVII × V
   e) Make up 3 of your own to scare your classmates. Make sure you work them out yourself too!

Place Value

As you can see, some of these numbers take up a lot of paper when written as Roman numerals. For example, there is no shorter way of writing 300 other than CCC. The Roman symbols have a specific value and not a <u>place value</u>, as in the system we use ourselves.

List all of the digits we use today, from which all numbers can be made:

0, 1, ____, ____, ____, ____, ____, ____, ____, ____

We use these digits, but to find out what number is being shown depends on the **place value** of the numbers. For example, what is the value of the 9 in each of these: 9, 90, 90, 9000?

The 9 does not change, but the **value** of the number depends on where it is **placed**.

3. What number is being shown on each notation board?

a)

Th	H	T	U

b)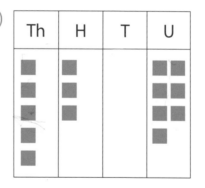

c)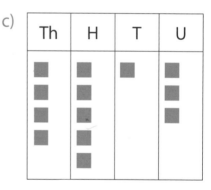

   d) What is the value of the digit 3 in each of the above notation boards?

4. Draw notation boards to show these numbers.
   a) 203   b) 1430   c) 9001   d) 706   e) 2034
   f) 3708   g) 199   h) 2040   i) 6053   j) 901

Think About

A new hotel has 100 rooms. The manager needs to buy numbers for all the doors. How many number 1s does she need to buy?

Of what number does she have to buy the least amount?

Now for Some Larger Numbers

13426 people attended a concert. What does each of these digits represent?

T Th	Th	H	T	U
●	● ● ●	● ● ● ●	● ●	● ● ● ● ● ●
1	**3**	**4**	**2**	**6**
1 ten thousand +	3 thousands +	4 hundreds +	2 tens +	6 units
= 10000 +	3000 +	400 +	20 +	6

You are playing a computer game and your top score is 15642. What is the value of the digit 1 in this number?

Fill in the rest of **15642** on the notation board.

T Th	Th	H	T	U
	● ● ● ● ●		● ● ● ●	

5. Draw notation boards to represent these large numbers.

   a) 17345   b) 12980   c) 16299   d) 10550

   e) 25120   f) 34611   g) 42810   h) 63452

6. What is the value of the underlined digit in each of the following?

   a) 687<u>5</u>   b) <u>2</u>3   c) 9<u>9</u>99   d) 28<u>1</u>

   e) <u>6</u>8   f) <u>8</u>008   g) 7<u>7</u>34   h) 38<u>0</u>

   i) 3<u>0</u>91   j) 6<u>5</u>6   k) <u>3</u>80   l) 10<u>2</u>37

m) 5<u>5</u>5   n) 92<u>0</u>3   o) 702<u>1</u>   p) 124<u>0</u>5

q) <u>9</u>020   r) 24<u>0</u>   s) 8<u>6</u>07   t) <u>2</u>350

7. Look at these 4 digits and answer the questions that follow.

5 0 8 2

a) What is the largest number you can make using all 4 digits?
b) What is the smallest number you can make using all 4 digits?
c) Write a number using all 4 digits with 8 in the hundreds position.
d) Write a number using all 4 digits with 5 in the tens position.
e) Write a number using all 4 digits with 0 in the units position.
f) Make the smallest even number using all 4 digits.
g) Make the largest odd number using all 4 digits.
h) Write a number greater than 8500.
i) Make up 3 more questions based on these numbers.

The Mysterious Briefcase

8. The briefcase the Garda found has a 3-digit code to open it. He knows that the 3 digits are **8 4 7** but he does not know the order of the numbers. Help him crack the code by writing down all the possibilities and so find the owner of the briefcase.

9. Here are some groups of 5 random digits. In each one, first make the largest number possible and then the smallest number possible.

a) 4 6 8 1 0   b) 3 2 0 8 1   c) 9 6 1 3 4

d) 0 3 5 7 2   e) 8 3 1 6 8   f) 5 3 4 1 1

g) 9 5 5 6 8   h) 3 5 1 9 3   i) 6 7 4 7 0

10. Guess the number!

9   4   7   1

a) Rearrange these digits and ask the person beside you to guess your number. The person knows the digits you have used but can only ask questions such as: Does your number have 4 hundreds? Is the unit an even number? You may only answer yes or no.

b) Try the same guessing game using these digits: **5 1 9 0 2**.

11. When you answer the top-secret red telephone, you are asked to write down some secret codes. Make sure you write down the numbers accurately!

a) Three hundred and thirty-seven
b) Four thousand, six hundred and twenty-nine
c) Five thousand and ninety-two
d) Ten thousand, eight hundred and seventy-one
e) Six thousand, three hundred and four

f) Fifteen thousand, two hundred

g) Sixty-eight thousand, one hundred and forty-five

h) One hundred thousand, three hundred and fifty-six

i) One hundred and fifty thousand, nine hundred and four

j) Two hundred and nineteen thousand, seven hundred and twelve

12. You now have to write these top-secret codes in words.

a) 524   b) 1670   c) 2043   d) 8927   e) 13460

f) 3409   g) 6710   h) 55234   i) 98125   j) 6089

k) 125390   l) 178200   m) 230461   n) 102308   o) 340087

13. Expand these numbers. The first one has been done for you.

a) $3491 = 3000 + 400 + 90 + 1$

b) $6280 =$

c) $9805 =$

d) $11236 =$

e) $25679 =$

f) $74035 =$

g) $138693 =$

h) $650431 =$

i) Write 5 of your own numbers and ask the person beside you to expand them.

14. Alan is looking to buy a new car and telephoned a few garages to get some prices. Write down the prices of each car in figures and then put them in order, starting with the most expensive.

a) Eight thousand, five hundred and fifty euro

b) Twelve thousand, nine hundred and ninety-nine euro

c) Ten thousand, four hundred and ten euro

d) Seventeen thousand and thirty euro

e) Twenty-five thousand, three hundred and five euro

f) Twenty-one thousand, eight hundred euro

Greater Than or Less Than

15. Insert the correct symbol < or > between each of these numbers.

a) 569 _____ 589   b) 725 _____ 527   c) 302 _____ 303

d) 745 _____ 475   e) 1460 _____ 1046   f) 2798 _____ 2978

g) 4520 _____ 5420   h) 7504 _____ 7405

i) 30456 _____ 30564   j) 17290 _____ 16290

16. Continue these sequences.

a) 15, 25, 35, 45, ____, ____, ____, ____, ____, ____, ____

b) 77, 87, 97, ____, ____, ____, ____, ____, ____, ____

c) 162, 152, ____, ____, ____, ____, ____, ____, ____

d) 279, 289, ____, ____, ____, ____, ____, ____, ____

e) 568, 558, ____, ____, ____, ____, ____, ____, ____

f) 1780, 1790, ____, ____, ____, ____, ____, ____, ____

g) 3230, 3220, ____, ____, ____, ____, ____, ____, ____

h) 448, 548, ____, ____, ____, ____, ____, ____, ____

i) 1870, 1770, ____, ____, ____, ____, ____, ____, ____

j) 2030, 3030, ____, ____, ____, ____, ____, ____, ____

k) 12420, 11420, ____, ____, ____, ____, ____, ____, ____

17. Work out the sequence and fill in the missing terms.

a) 570, 600, 630, ____, 690, ____, ____, 780, ____, ____

b) 125, 185, ____, ____, 365, 425, ____, ____, ____, 665

c) 348, ____, 388, 408, ____, ____, 468, ____, ____, ____

d) 780, 730, ____, ____, ____, 530, 480, ____, ____, ____

e) 213, ____, 413, ____, 613, 713, ____, ____, ____, 1113

f) 1420, 1445, 1470, ____, ____, 1545, ____, ____, ____, 1645

18. Here are the Lottery numbers as they came out of the drum for the past 8 draws.
Put the numbers in order, starting with the smallest, before they are sent to the newspapers.

a) 39, 42, 10, 7, 28, 8   b) 30, 4, 5, 2, 34, 12

c) 27, 35, 42, 4, 5, 29   d) 11, 4, 41, 22, 20, 14

e) 9, 15, 32, 39, 13, 17   f) 7, 14, 1, 12, 32, 25

g) 15, 4, 27, 29, 17, 32   h) 34, 22, 40, 9, 2, 14

19. For some unknown reason, when printing tickets for the past few weeks, the Lottery machine has been adding 1000 to every number.

a) Can you add 1000 to each of the above numbers?

b) Does it change the order of the numbers?

20. Write these numbers in order, starting with the largest.

a) 15, 55, 505, 5, 500, 5550, 105, 525

b) 202, 2102, 22, 2120, 2000, 210, 12, 200

c) 6340, 6370, 637, 4370, 76430, 6347, 673

d) 5240, 55240, 4520, 450, 55, 340, 2530, 45

e) 9865, 98650, 986, 896, 8566, 6579, 5768

f) 5006, 6005, 6050, 50060, 66500, 65600

21. **20560**

What number is   a) 1000 greater   b) 1000 less   c) 10000 greater?

65120

What number is   d) 100 greater   e) 100 less   f) 10000 less?

Calculating Calculator

Figure out the difference between the first 2 numbers by keying it into the calculator and repeatedly pressing the = sign. Watch what happens!

$$15980, 14480, \rule{2cm}{0.4pt}, \rule{2cm}{0.4pt}, \rule{2cm}{0.4pt} \ldots$$

15980 − 1500 = 14480, so key in 15980 − 1500 = = = = to fill in the sequence. Try it out!

Note: this may not work on every calculator.

22. Use your calculator to complete these sequences.

a) 25898, 23898, _____, _____, _____, _____, _____, _____

b) 50620, 47120, _____, _____, _____, _____, _____, _____

c) 46200, 42200, _____, _____, _____, _____, _____, _____

d) 60150, 54150, _____, _____, _____, _____, _____, _____

e) 28640, 28840, _____, _____, _____, _____, _____, _____

f) Invent 3 similar sequences with your calculator and record them.

23. What number am I?

a) I am a 5-digit number. 4 of my digits are zeros and I am the largest number possible with those 4 zeros.

b) I am a 3-digit number greater than 350 but less than 400. All of my digits are odd and the sum of my digits is 9.

c) I am a 5-digit number. There is a 1 in my ten thousands place. I am the largest number I can be.

d) I am a 4-digit number. If you add 1 to this number I will be a 5-digit number.

e) I am a 5-digit number. There is a 3 in my hundreds place and my number reads the same backwards and forwards. The sum of the digits is 9. Is there more than 1 answer?

24. a) Complete this multiplication table.

×	10	100	1000
5			
	80		
10			
		1200	
16			
23			
34			
			51,000
70			
95			

b) Examine the chart and then come up with a rule for multiplying by 10, 100 and 1000.

25. Divide each of the following numbers by 10 and by 100.

a) 3200 b) 4500 c) 9000 d) 1500 e) 2000

f) 6100 g) 7600 h) 12000 i) 5900 j) 18000

26. Sharon is a bit confused. When writing down a series of numbers, she wrote them all 10 times too big. Help her correct her mistake by dividing each of the numbers by 10.

a) 640 b) 1200 c) 3520 d) 8090

e) 1440 f) 6700 g) 6690 h) 13780

i) 98130 j) 26700 k) 50110 l) 78020

m) 82600 n) 130560 o) 250900

27. Fill in this division table.

÷	4100	6200		9600		10300	17400	19800
÷ 10			730					
÷ 100					84			

As with whole numbers, place value is very important when dealing with decimals. The decimal point separates the whole numbers from the fractions.

So in the number 34.25, what does each of the numbers represent?

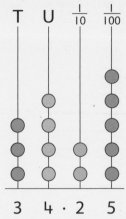

$$3 \quad 4 \cdot 2 \quad 5$$

3 tens + 4 units + 2 tenths + 5 hundredths

$$= \quad 30 \quad + \quad 4 \quad + \quad \frac{2}{10} \quad + \quad \frac{5}{100}$$

28. Fill in the following decimal on the notation board: 31.24.

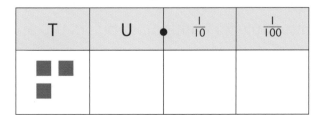

29. Draw notation boards to represent each of these numbers.
    a) 20.15   b) 38.91   c) 16.23   d) 69.34   e) 28.3
    f) 70.5   g) 125.67   h) 230.41   i) 456.2

30. In the following decimals, write down whether the underlined digit is a hundred, ten, unit, tenth or hundredth.
    a) 23.46   b) 981.5   c) 62.12   d) 334.6   e) 25.99
    f) 698.07   g) 54.29   h) 708.42   i) 459.1   j) 80.27
    k) 158.39   l) 6.7   m) 500.03   n) 783.15   o) 480.29

31. Which of the following decimals are between the numbers 1 and 2? Draw a number line and mark the numbers on it to help you.
    a) 1.1   b) 0.5   c) 1.8   d) 1.25
    e) 2.3   f) 1.7   g) 2.6   h) 1.54

32. Fill in the missing decimals on the following number lines.

    4.3   4.8

    a)

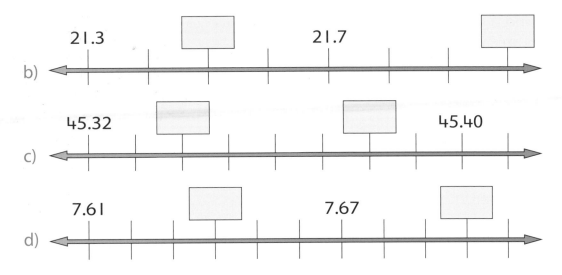

b) 21.3 ▢ 21.7 ▢

c) 45.32 ▢ ▢ 45.40

d) 7.61 ▢ 7.67 ▢

33. Which number from the list is the closest to each of the bold numbers?

a) **4.7**: 5.7, 4.8, 5.0
b) **6.1**: 6.3, 7.0, 5.5
c) **12.5**: 12.9, 12.4, 13.5
d) **36.3**: 36.4, 37.1, 35.3
e) **6.35**: 6.4, 6.36, 7.3
f) **10.12**: 11.12, 10.22, 10.11
g) **17.82**: 17.12, 17.83, 18.1
h) **63.55**: 63.54, 63.6, 63.1

34. Continue these sequences.

a) 3.1, 3.2, 3.3, _____, _____, _____, _____, _____, _____, _____, _____

b) 8.6, 8.7, 8.8, _____, _____, _____, _____, _____, _____, _____, _____

c) 14.5, 14.6, _____, _____, _____, _____, _____, _____, _____, _____

d) 28.6, 28.5, _____, _____, _____, _____, _____, _____, _____, _____

e) 79.9, 79.6, _____, _____, _____, _____, _____, _____, _____, _____

f) 166.6, 166.4, _____, _____, _____, _____, _____, _____

g) 478.3, 478.5, _____, _____, _____, _____, _____, _____

h) 37.46, 37.47, _____, _____, _____, _____, _____, _____

i) 69.35, 69.34, _____, _____, _____, _____, _____, _____

j) 130.78, 130.68, _____, _____, _____, _____, _____, _____

k) 563.11, 563.14, _____, _____, _____, _____, _____, _____

35. A comparison was made between the same item in a number of different shops. List the prices of the items in order, starting with the cheapest.

a) Orange juice: €1.59, €1.55, €1.62, €1.50, €1.49, €1.45
b) Bread: €0.85, €0.75, €0.89, €0.90, €0.82, €0.80
c) Pasta: €1.45, €1.47, €1.40, €1.52, €1.39, €1.50
d) Lemonade: €1.60, €1.55, €1.73, €1.70, €1.82, €1.65
e) Biscuits: €1.39, €1.45, €1.40, €1.59, €1.55, €1.65
f) Shower gel: €2.29, €2.41, €2.36, €2.60, €2.35, €2.75
g) Lettuce: €0.45, €0.55, €0.46, €0.49, €0.52, €0.60

36. Sally is organising a party and is ringing different places to find out the entrance fees per person. Take down the prices for her, making sure to use the decimal point.

   a) Bowling: Six euro and fifty-five cent
   b) Swimming: One euro and ninety-five cent
   c) Quasar: Eight euro and sixty cent
   d) Fun fair: Ten euro and seventy-nine cent
   e) Put the prices in order, starting with the most expensive.

Rounding to the Nearest Ten

As we learned in 3rd class, if you are asked to round a number to the nearest ten, you must say the multiple of ten that is nearest to that number. (Multiples of ten are 10, 20, 30, 40, 50, 60 and so on.)

It helps to look at a number line.

For example: Round 32 to the nearest ten.

29 30 31 32 33 34 35 36 37 38 39 40 41

Look at where 32 is on the number line. Which multiple of ten is it nearer to, 30 or 40?

It is nearer to 30. Therefore, 32 rounds down to the nearest ten, which is 30.

Note:
- Numbers 31, 32, 33 and 34 round down to 30 because they are nearer to 30 than 40.
- Numbers 36, 37, 38 and 39 round up to 40 because they are nearer to 40 than 30.
- Number 35 is exactly halfway between 30 and 40. The rule in this case is to round up to 40.

1. Estimate the following to the nearest ten.
   a) children in your class   b) items in your pencil case
   c) books on your table   d) paintbrushes in your classroom
   e) pages in your maths copy   f) pages in this book

2. Round these numbers to the nearest ten.
   a) 7   b) 15   c) 9   d) 4   e) 33
   f) 35   g) 27   h) 49   i) 52   j) 98
   k) 116   l) 142   m) 256   n) 948   o) 4678

3. Barry is counting how many marbles he has altogether. He has 7 different types of marbles, each in their own bag.

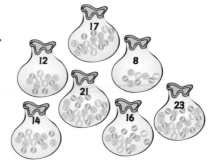

   a) Estimate how many marbles Barry has altogether by rounding the number in each bag to the nearest ten.

   b) Check how close your answer was by adding the amount of marbles in each bag.

4. Have a go at rounding these numbers to the nearest ten.
   (Hint: no matter how big the number is, when rounding to the nearest ten you only need to look at the units.)

   a) 788   b) 543   c) 244   d) 607   e) 986

   f) 3461   g) 1708   h) 2516   i) 15355   j) 71348

5. Rounding Riddles – what number am I?

   a) I am a multiple of 9 and am 40 when rounded to the nearest ten.

   b) I am the number of months in the year rounded to the nearest ten.

   c) I am the number of days in the year rounded to the nearest ten.

   d) I am the number of holes on a golf course rounded to the nearest ten.

   e) Invent 3 of your own Rounding Riddles.

Rounding to the Nearest Hundred

As we learned in 4th class, if you are asked to round a number to the nearest hundred, you must say the multiple of one hundred that is nearest to that number. (Multiples of one hundred are 100, 200, 300, 400, 500, 600 and so on.)

It helps to look at a number line.

For example: Round 475 to the nearest hundred.

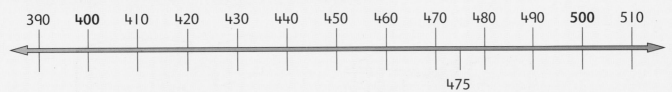

Look at where 475 is on the number line. Which multiple of one hundred is it nearer to, 400 or 500?

It is nearer to 500. Therefore, 475 rounds up to the nearest hundred, which is 500.

When rounding in hundreds, if there are **less than five tens**, **we round down** to the nearest hundred, but if there are **five tens or more**, **we round up** to the nearest hundred.

Note:
- Numbers 401 to 449 round down to 400 because they are nearer to 400 than 500.
- Numbers 451 to 499 round up to 500 because they are nearer to 500 than 400.
- Number 450 is exactly halfway between 400 and 500. The rule in this case is to round up to 500.

1. Round these numbers to the nearest hundred.
   a) 65   b) 71   c) 80   d) 126   e) 142
   f) 155   g) 213   h) 179   i) 262   j) 420
   k) 346   l) 350   m) 677   n) 1360   o) 1685
   p) 2806   q) 4216   r) 8935   s) 12578   t) 35121

2. The cinema in town holds a maximum of 500 people.
   a) Estimate how many people went to the cinema this week by rounding the
      number of tickets sold for each night to the nearest hundred and adding them.

Day	Number of Tickets Sold
Monday	172
Tuesday	243
Wednesday	312
Thursday	361
Friday	445
Saturday	476
Sunday	413

   b) Exactly how many people went to the cinema in the town this week?

3. Estimate the answers to these by rounding the numbers to the nearest hundred and
   then working them out.
   a) 570 + 310   b) 124 + 780   c) 1352 + 1679
   d) 830 – 288   e) 487 – 190   f) 5299 – 1430

4. Maura's mum is buying a few new household appliances. She needs a rough estimate
   of how much money she will need. Round these prices to the nearest hundred and
   add them to give her that estimate.

€469

€230

€289

€175

Rounding to the Nearest Thousand

If you are asked to round a number to the nearest thousand, you must say the multiple of one thousand that is nearest to that number. (Multiples of one thousand are 1000, 2000, 3000, 4000, 5000, 6000 and so on.)

Again, it helps to look at a number line.

For example: Round 5670 to the nearest thousand.

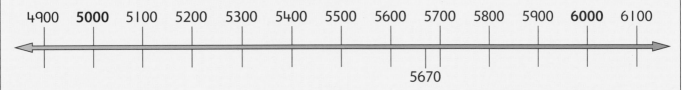

Look at where 5670 is on the number line. Which multiple of 1000 is it nearer to, 5000 or 6000?

It is nearer to 6000. Therefore, 5670 rounds up to the nearest thousand, which is 6000.

When rounding in thousands, if there are **less than five hundreds, we round down** to the nearest thousand, but if there are **five hundreds or more, we round up** to the nearest thousand.

Note:
- Numbers 5001 to 5499 round down to 5000 because they are nearer to 5000 than 6000.
- Numbers 5501 to 5999 round up to 6000 because they are nearer to 6000 than 5000.
- Number 5500 is exactly halfway between 5000 and 6000. The rule in this case is to round up to 6000.

1. Round these numbers to the nearest thousand.

   a) 1230   b) 890   c) 1765   d) 2879   e) 1340
   f) 2545   g) 4060   h) 6721   i) 3650   j) 5167
   k) 3390   l) 9880   m) 8290   n) 10380   o) 12860
   p) 31400   q) 56760   r) 28100   s) 40650   t) 93310

2. Karl is buying a new car. He has found 4 cars he likes and needs to have a look at the prices. Round each price to the nearest thousand and put them in order, starting with the most expensive.

€19900

€12450

€14300

€10999

3. Estimate the answers to these by rounding the numbers to the nearest thousand and then working them out.

   a) 2780 + 4200   b) 3480 + 1930   c) 7600 + 5130

   d) 8765 + 9410   e) 9200 − 4760   f) 6456 − 2895

4. Which is nearer to the number in bold? Estimate first, then check your answers.

   a) **10**: 7 or 14   b) **100**: 56 or 145

   c) **300**: 278 or 320   d) **5000**: 4328 or 5675

   e) **50000**: 48130 or 51800   f) **100000**: 96500 or 104500

Rounding Decimals to the Nearest Whole Number

If you are asked to round a decimal to the nearest whole number, you must say the whole number that is nearest to that number.

It helps to look at a number line.

For example: Round 2.3 to the nearest whole number.

Look at where 2.3 is on the number line. To which whole number is it nearer, 2 or 3?

It is nearer to 2. Therefore, 2.3 rounds down to the nearest whole number, which is 2.

Note:

- Numbers 2.1, 2.2, 2.3 and 2.4 round down to 2 because they are nearer to 2 than 3.
- Numbers 2.6, 2.7, 2.8 and 2.9 round up to 3 because they are nearer to 3 than 2.
- Number 2.5 is exactly halfway between 2 and 3. The rule in this case is to round up to 3.

5. Round these decimals to the nearest whole number.

   a) 4.7   b) 3.1   c) 8.6   d) 5.4   e) 9.8

   f) 12.2   g) 23.9   h) 38.2   i) 43.5   j) 57.4

   k) 68.6   l) 89.8   m) 96.5   n) 109.1   o) 112.7

When rounding decimals to the nearest whole number, we only need to look at the tenths. If there are five tenths or more, we round up, but if there are less than five tenths, we round down.

For example: Round 15.258 to the nearest whole number.

15.258 is between 15 and 16. The 2 in the tenths place is less than 5, so we round down to the lower whole number, which is 15.

6. Round these decimals to the nearest whole number.
   a) 1.74   b) 11.38   c) 25.96   d) 31.19   e) 45.82
   f) 4.593   g) 7.278   h) 10.601   i) 19.459   j) 63.286
   k) 47.81   l) 142.375   m) 0.92   n) 5.188   o) 29.51
   p) 403.6   q) 17.489   r) 253.27   s) 8.911   t) 56.06

Homework

1. Draw notation boards to show these numbers.
   a) 748   b) 2083   c) 7106   d) 405   e) 6274
   f) 9316   g) 19275   h) 31008   i) 28667   j) 40708

2. What is the value of the underlined digit?
   a) 2406   b) 51   c) 3592   d) 17682   e) 95
   f) 3020   g) 8226   h) 876   i) 23271   j) 1908
   k) 45234   l) 17488   m) 4824   n) 81773   o) 6555

3. Write these numbers in words.
   a) 736   b) 7421   c) 19543   d) 11902   e) 8274
   f) 24016   g) 6003   h) 39108   i) 74169   j) 2017

4. Work out the sequence and fill in the missing terms.
   a) 240, 280, 320, _____, 400, _____, _____, 520, _____, _____
   b) 415, 385, _____, _____, 295, 265, _____, _____, _____
   c) 323, _____, 463, 533, 603, _____, 743, _____
   d) 902, 857, 812, _____, _____, 677, 632, _____, _____
   e) 234, 344, 454, _____, _____, _____, _____
   f) 1105, 1030, _____, 880, 805, _____, _____, _____

5. Divide each of these numbers by 10 and 100.
   a) 11000   b) 7300   c) 23800   d) 14000   e) 1900
   f) 34300   g) 5100   h) 16800   i) 2800   j) 52200

6. Draw notation boards to represent each of these numbers.
   a) 5.94   b) 27.03   c) 41.27
   d) 20.5   e) 7.08   f) 80.38

7. In the following decimals, write down whether the underlined digit is a hundred, ten, unit, tenth or hundredth.

   a) 72.<u>9</u>   b) 42.0<u>8</u>   c) 2<u>9</u>5.7   d) <u>2</u>75.86   e) 53.<u>6</u>

   f) 937.2<u>4</u>   g) <u>1</u>.02   h) <u>5</u>14.7   i) <u>3</u>4.34   j) 100.2<u>9</u>

8. Round these numbers to the nearest ten.

   a) 8   b) 21   c) 44   d) 69   e) 96

   f) 104   g) 248   h) 813   i) 566   j) 975

   k) 1023   l) 2347   m) 3819   n) 7898   o) 9253

9. Round these numbers to the nearest hundred.

   a) 59   b) 134   c) 151   d) 280   e) 312

   f) 461   g) 548   h) 605   i) 777   j) 939

   k) 1007   l) 1267   m) 1817   n) 3542   o) 7298

10. Round these numbers to the nearest thousand.

   a) 1144   b) 1456   c) 1920   d) 2508   e) 3612

   f) 4019   g) 6721   h) 6324   i) 7705   j) 8293

   k) 8967   l) 9562   m) 12431   n) 25680   o) 49800

11. Round these decimals to the nearest whole number.

   a) 2.9   b) 8.3   c) 12.5   d) 7.26   e) 19.59

   f) 6.713   g) 28.019   h) 76.498   i) 2.75   j) 90.62

   k) 409.39   l) 280.53   m) 39.268   n) 32.05   o) 539.81

Recap

- I can read write and order whole numbers.   ◯ ◯ ◯

- I can multiply and divide whole numbers by 10/100/1000.   ◯ ◯ ◯

- I can read, write and order decimals.   ◯ ◯ ◯

- I can round whole numbers to the nearest 10/100/1000.   ◯ ◯ ◯

3. Operations 1

Think About

Choose which is the 'best' number to use in each of the following statements. You may need to do some estimating and some research.

1) There are roughly 10 million / 200 million / 1000 million domestic cats in the world.

2) On average, cats weigh 1.5 / 4.5 / 8kg.

3) On average, domestic cats sleep 8–9 / 13–14 / 18–19 hours a day.

Estimates

Guess the answers to these questions.

a) What will the weather be like in 5 minutes?

b) What colour socks is your teacher wearing?

c) Will the next person to enter the classroom be male or female?

d) Without looking at a watch or a clock, how long is left until lunchtime?

e) Who is the youngest person in the class?

Discuss your answers with the people near you.

Some guesses are easier to make than others. Why do you think that is?

We make better guesses by looking more closely at the question and by looking for clues.

For example, in the question about the weather, if the sun is shining and there isn't a cloud in the sky, it is more than likely that in 5 minutes the sun will still be shining.

If we are asked to guess the answer to a sum, we can make an informed guess or **estimate** by looking for clues in the sum.

Strand: Number
Curriculum Objectives:
Estimate sums and differences of whole numbers;
add and subtract whole numbers without and with a calculator.

21

John went into a bookshop and bought 4 books priced €1.94, €2.10, €2.83 and €3.16. Estimate how much money he spent in the bookshop.

Estimate 1

Ignore the cent and just add the euro to get a euro estimate:

$1 + 2 + 2 + 3 =$

Estimate 2

Look at the cent amount in each case: 94, 10, 83, 16. Combine the cent amounts that nearly make full euros to get a cent estimate. Then add in your answer from **estimate 1** to get an adjusted estimate.

> **cent estimate + euro estimate = estimate 2**

Estimate 3

Round the prices of the books up or down to the nearest euro. For example, €1.94 is nearer to €2 than it is to €1. Do the same for the other amounts and then add to get your estimate.

Estimate 4

Rather than just add, look for numbers that when combined give you a number that is easier to work with when estimating. For example, 83 + 16 is almost 100.

Now add the book prices and find out what John actually spent.

```
   1.94
   2.10
   2.83
+  3.16
_____
```

Which method of estimating is usually going to be the least accurate? Explain why.

1. Now estimate the answers to these sums. Choose whatever method of estimating you think is most appropriate to the sum. You do not have to actually add the sums.

> **Remember:** an estimate cannot be right or wrong – it is just that some estimates are closer than others.

a)	b)	c)	d)	e)	f)
2.89	5.17	11.97	15.49	27.16	41.03
4.12	2.23	6.05	24.52	23.90	7.18
+ 1.53	+ 4.62	+ 0.79	+ 19.88	+ 25.34	+ 53.68

g) €1983 + €3015 + €975 =

h) €7791 + €4210 + €5598 =

i) €11007 + €9989 + €16599 =

j) €22890 + €17063 + €25194 =

Adding Bigger Numbers

1. A group of friends had a competition with their favourite computer game, Days of Doom, to see which of them would have the highest aggregate score over 3 games. In each case, estimate the aggregate score first, then add the numbers to see how accurate your estimate is. Use your calculator to check your answers.

Game	Nathan	Hannah	Finola	Dylan	James	Sarah
1	1795	5929	19827	1006	4192	12495
2	2031	21604	22104	8912	10043	15012
3	17200	3031	6008	9183	2809	11508

2. When Hannah went to bed, her mum and dad had a go at the game as well. See if you can do the same with their scores.

Game	1	2	3
Mum	329	6487	91
Dad	4653	2098	34

Use your calculator to find the answers to the following problems.

3. Find the sum of 15436 and 29078.

4. While training for the school sports, Tom ran a distance of 12479 metres on Monday. On Tuesday he increased that distance by 2138 metres. How far did he run on Tuesday? How far did he run over the 2 days?

5. At a music festival, 21543 attended on the Friday, 27936 attended on Saturday and 23458 attended on Sunday. How many people attended the festival altogether?

6. Add the number of people in the class, the number of days in the year and the number of seconds in an hour.

We can use most of the same methods to estimate when we are subtracting. Use the first 3 ways of estimating to get different estimates for this problem:

Jane had €87.03 in her bank account. She withdrew €19.95. How much was left in the account?

Subtracting Bigger Numbers

In 2008, the population of a city was 8875. By 2013, the population had risen to 11364. By how much had the population risen?

First Step

We look at the units column first.

We cannot take 5 units from 4 units, so we must rename a ten from the tens column.

The 6 tens become 5 tens and we now have 14 units.

We can now work out the units column (14 − 5 = 9), so we write down 9 as our answer in the units column.

T Th	Th	H	T	U
1	1	3	⁵6̷	¹4
−		8	8	7	5
				9

Second Step

We look at the tens column next.

We cannot take 7 tens from 5 tens, so we must rename a hundred from the hundreds column.

The 3 hundreds become 2 hundreds and we now have 15 tens.

We can now work out the tens column (15 − 7 = 8), so we write down 8 as our answer in the tens column.

T Th	Th	H	T	U
1	1	²3̷	¹⁵6̷	¹4
−		8	8	7	5
			8	9

Third Step

We look at the hundreds column next.

We cannot take 8 hundreds from 2 hundreds, so we must rename a thousand from the thousands column.

The 1 thousand becomes 0 thousands and we now have 12 hundreds.

We can now work out the hundreds column (12 − 8 = 4), so we write down 4 as our answer in the hundreds column.

T Th	Th	H	T	U
1	⁰1̷	¹²3̷	¹⁵6̷	¹4
−		8	8	7	5
		4	8	9

Fourth Step

We look at the thousands column next.

We cannot take 8 thousands from 0 thousands, so we must rename a ten thousand from the ten thousands column.

The 1 ten thousand becomes 0 ten thousands and we now have 10 thousands.

We can now work out the thousands column (10 − 8 = 2), so we write down 2 as our answer in the thousands column.

T Th	Th	H	T	U
⁰1̷	¹⁰1̷	¹²3̷	¹⁵6̷	¹4
−		8	8	7	5
	2	4	8	9

As there is nothing left in the ten thousands column and nothing to take away, we are finished subtracting. So the population of the city has grown by 2489.

1. Estimate the amounts left in these people's bank accounts after they made withdrawals. Use whatever method you feel works best.

Account	Tim	Tom	Ted	Tess	Tina	Teri
Opening balance	92.13	59.29	190.07	107.08	41.92	172.15
Amount withdrawn	54.91	30.31	63.78	91.83	28.09	145.86
Closing balance						

2. Estimate the answers to each of the following and then work out the answers to see how accurate your estimate was. Use your calculator to check your answers.

a) 4012
   − 1536

b) 8233
   − 4627

c) 6051
   − 5798

d) 2002
   − 1988

e) 12390
   − 2534

f) 10782
   − 5368

g) 3591 − 1285 =

h) 9016 − 878 =

i) 5193 − 3629 =

j) 13305 − 7664 =

k) 18008 − 14237 =

l) 21102 − 12556 =

3. Anne's top score on a computer game is 34934 and Joe's top score is 18238. What is the difference between their scores?

4. If 45697 tickets were sold for a football match but only 38729 people actually attended, how many people did not use their tickets?

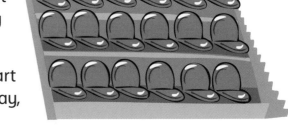

5. €20000 was placed in a bank machine at the start of the day. If €13290 was taken out during the day, how much money was left in the machine?

6. This table shows the number of people who went to these countries on their holidays. Work out the answers to the following questions.

Holiday destinations	2012	2013
Italy	16945	13679
Spain	33527	29258
Portugal	18638	21310
France	27092	25432
United Kingdom	23445	28719

a) Which was the most popular destination in 2012?

b) Which was the least popular destination in 2013?

c) How many people went to Portugal over the 2 years?

d) How many fewer people went to France in 2013 than in 2012?

e) How many more people went to the United Kingdom in 2013 than in 2012?

f) What is the total number of people who travelled to Spain and Italy over the 2 years?

g) If the number going to Italy in 2014 increases by 3978 from 2013, how many people will travel to Italy in 2014?

h) If the number going to France in 2014 decreases by 1379 from 2013, how many people will travel to France in 2014?

Another Way to Estimate

There are 31 children in a class. The attendance for the week was as follows:

Monday – 29, Tuesday – 30, Wednesday – 31, Thursday – 31, Friday – 29

Estimate the total attendance for the week.

When all of the numbers are either just above or just below a certain number, then we can round all the numbers up or down to the same number – in this case, 30.

So a good estimate would be 30 + 30 + 30 + 30 + 30 = 150.

But a quicker way of doing repeated addition is multiplication. Write out the new estimate.

Estimate the answers to the following questions before working them out to see how accurate your estimate was.

7. Alan weighs 48kg, Michael weighs 51kg and Frank weighs 49kg. What is their total weight?

8. Anne, Paula, Gemma and Laura went to the cinema. Before going in to see the film they each bought a pick and mix bag of sweets. Anne's cost €1.25, Paula's cost €1.35, Gemma's cost €1.28 and Laura's cost €1.33. Laura bought the sweets for everyone. How much did the sweets cost?

9. How many days are there in spring?

10. During the course of a week, a woman drove the following distances each day: 195km, 208km, 203km, 189km, 212km, 207km and 191km. What was the total distance driven in the week?

Homework

1. Estimate the answers to these and then work out the answers to see how accurate your estimate was. Use your calculator to check your answers.

a)	b)	c)	d)	e)	f)
309	488	1208	1652	3415	2295
294	313	597	3447	5587	689
+ 248	+ 153	+ 179	+ 4006	+ 1791	+ 6702

g) €2012 + €1478 + €986 =   h) €5604 + €3392 + €4489 =

i) €9986 + €10006 + €14692 =   j) €17705 + €26294 + €29412 =

2. Estimate the answers to these and then work out the answers to see how accurate your estimate was. Use your calculator to check your answers.

a)	b)	c)	d)	e)	f)
2294	5311	8349	9007	11504	16693
− 1608	− 2789	− 4353	− 7898	− 8479	− 12718

g) 7396 − 4414 =   h) 8007 − 5196 =   i) 9205 − 786 =

j) 12411 − 8592 =   k) 16015 − 12694 =   l) 25208 − 16589 =

3. The following table shows the votes 4 candidates received in an election. Each candidate received transfers from other candidates to increase their vote in count 2. Answer the questions based on the table.

Candidate	Count 1	Count 2
Tom Thomas	9037	10354
Lucy Lucey	11269	12045
Phil Phillips	10765	11416
Carol O'Carroll	8932	11681

a) Which candidate had the greatest increase in votes from count 1 to count 2?

b) What was the difference in votes between Lucy Lucey and Carol O'Carroll after count 1 and after count 2?

c) Which candidate received the fewest number of transfers from count 1 to count 2?

d) What is the difference between each of the candidates after count 2?

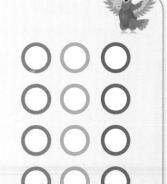

Recap

· I can estimate and calculate totals.   ◯ ◯ ◯

· I can use a calculator to check totals.   ◯ ◯ ◯

· I can estimate and calculate differences.   ◯ ◯ ◯

· I can use multiplication to estimate totals.   ◯ ◯ ◯

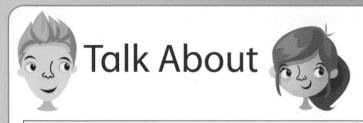

Talk About

Using 2 rows of pegs, arrange 7 pegs on a pegboard. The first 4 pegs have been done for you.

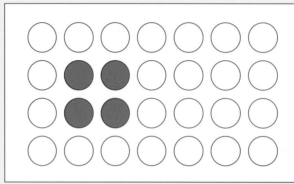

Using 2 rows of pegs, arrange the following numbers on your pegboard.

6   9   13   16   12   19

What do you notice about your results?

Now divide each of these numbers by 2 and compare your answers with how they are arranged on the pegboard.

Group the numbers into categories depending on your findings. What would you call these categories? Discuss it with the people near you. Try some numbers of your own and see which group they belong to.

Odd or Even?

When you divide a number by 2, if there is no remainder it is called an even number. If there is a remainder, it is called an odd number.

1. Put a circle around each of the odd numbers in this list of numbers.

12	17	5	10	21	27
34	103	56	79	98	45

Strand: Number
Curriculum Objectives:
Identify factors and multiples.

Factors and Products

What number does this arrangement of coloured squares represent?

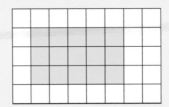

They are arranged in 3 rows of 5, so we can write it as 3 × 5.

3 and 5 are called **factors** of 15 because when multiplied together, they **make** 15.

We call 15 the **product** of the factors.
So **factor × factor = product**.

Could we arrange 15 in any other way?

> Did you know that the word **factor** means 'doer' or 'maker'?

1. In your copy, arrange these numbers into rows of coloured squares that show their factors. Write the number at the top and the factors underneath.

| 8 | 10 | 21 | 35 |
| 14 | 11 | 9 | 17 |

Prime Numbers and Composite Numbers

What do you notice about 11 and 17? Discuss it with the people near you.

What can we say about the factors of 11 and 17? Can you think of any other numbers like 11 and 17? Make a list of them in your copy as you think of new ones.

We call these numbers **prime numbers**.

Make up a sentence that says exactly what a prime number is. You must use the word **factors** in the sentence.

A prime number is a number that _____.

All of the other numbers in the exercise above have more than 1 set of factors. If we look at 8:

$$1 × 8 = 8 \text{ and } 2 × 4 = 8$$

So 8 has more factors than just itself and 1. We call numbers like these **composite numbers**. Can you guess why?

1. Arrange these composite numbers into rows of coloured squares in your copy. Write their factors underneath them.

| 12 | 18 | 20 | 24 | 28 | 36 |

2. Make these statements true by filling in the blanks.

   a) All numbers are either _____ numbers or _____ numbers.

   b) All numbers that are prime cannot be _____.

   c) All numbers that are composite cannot be _____.

3. Put a circle around the odd number out in each of these lists of numbers. You must be able to explain why it's the odd one out.

   a) 5, 13, 23, 9, 37   b) 6, 24, 39, 17, 36

   c) 27, 33, 11, 45, 15   d) 41, 57, 61, 83, 97

   Now fill in this table. The first one has been done for you.

Number	Prime / Composite	Factors
7	Prime	1 × 7
12		
19		
20		
27		
43		
33		
37		

4. Can you write all the factors of 16 in a list? The first 2 have been done for you.

   1, 2, ____, ____, ____

5. Now write all of the factors of the following products in a list. (Hint: start with 1.)

   a) 18   b) 22   c) 12   d) 11

   e) 24   f) 20   g) 49   h) 30

What did you notice about the factors of 30?

If a number is even, then _____ will always be a factor.

You can use your calculator to find out if smaller numbers like 3 and 4 are factors of larger numbers.

Try it to see if 3 and 4 are factors of these numbers.

Place a ✓ or an ✗ in each of the boxes to show whether or not they are factors.

Number	3	4
54		
68		
94		
76		
81		
108		

6. Now see if you can write the lists of factors of these numbers. Remember: there might be some factors you haven't considered. Use your calculator to help you.

a) 28   b) 36   c) 40   d) 38

e) 45   f) 42   g) 64   h) 100

> We can already see that every list of factors begins with 1. So 1 is a factor **common** to all products.

7. List the factors of 12 and 16.

12 = 1, ____, ____, ____, ____, ____

16 = 1, ____, ____, ____, ____

> Put a circle around all of the factors that appear on both lists in question 7.
> **These are called common factors.**

8. Do the same thing for the following pairs of products. Don't forget to circle the factors they have in common.

a) 8 and 10   b) 9 and 15   c) 14 and 21

d) 16 and 24   e) 9 and 18   f) 20 and 40

Multiples

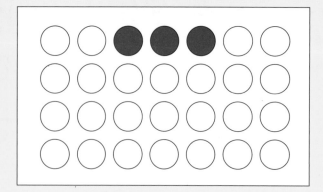

Put another row of 3 pegs underneath the blue pegs and record the new number.
Place further rows of 3 pegs and record the numbers each time.

1 row of 3 = 1 × **3** = 3
2 rows of 3 = 2 × **3** =

Keep going.

All of these **multiplications** have the number **3** in them. We call the answers to these **multiples of 3**.

This time, use the squares in your copy to draw and record some of the multiples of 5.
In your own words, say what you think a multiple is:

A multiple is _____ .

Your teacher can judge to see whose explanation is best. (There might even be a prize!)

What are the first 5 multiples of 4?

  1 × 4 =
  2 × 4 =
  3 × 4 =
  4 × 4 =
  5 × 4 =

The answers to these multiplications will be the first 5 multiples of 4.
Write them out as a list.

Now write the next 5 multiples of 4 without doing the multiplication.

---

1. Make lists of the following.

   a) The first 7 multiples of 3
   b) The first 4 multiples of 12
   c) The first 5 multiples of 8
   d) The first 8 multiples of 7
   e) The first 6 multiples of 9
   f) The first 9 multiples of 5

2. Is it possible to write the complete list of multiples of a number? Explain your answer.

Puzzler

Chloe has a clothes shop. She sells shirts for €48, trousers for €64 and a tie for €24, for a particular mathematical reason.

What would she charge for socks?

3. Pick the odd number out in each of these lists of numbers. You must be able to give a reason for your answer.

   a) 28, 49, 44, 42, 63, 84

   b) 48, 32, 12, 42, 54, 72

   c) 21, 33, 132, 88, 121

   d) 56, 36, 66, 98, 25, 100

Is 51 a multiple of 3? There are 3 ways of finding out.

Firstly, we could write out all the multiples of 3 up as far as 51 to see if it appears on the list:

3, 6, 9, 12, 15, 18, 21, 24, 27, 30, 33 …

That could take a while. (Imagine if we had been asked if 351 was a multiple of 3!)

There is a quicker way. If 3 divides into 51 evenly, then we know that 51 is a multiple of 3. Try it:

$$3\overline{)51}$$

But there is an even quicker way: use your calculator to see if 3 divides evenly into 51.

---

4. Use your calculator to find out whether these statements are true or false.

   a) 96 is a multiple of 4

   b) 254 is a multiple of 8

   c) 107 is a multiple of 3

   d) 588 is a multiple of 12

   e) 475 is a multiple of 9

   f) 651 is a multiple of 7

How would we know without dividing if a number is a multiple of 5?

5. a) Put a circle around all the multiples of 4 in this list: 324, 158, 476, 734

   b) Put a circle around all the multiples of 6 in this list: 548, 732, 834, 918

   c) Put a circle around all the multiples of 9 in this list: 378, 504, 458, 763

   d) Put a circle around all the multiples of 11 in this list: 547, 198, 642, 935

Homework

1. Circle the even numbers in the following list of numbers.

15	24	9	48	37	2
39	81	66	73	52	108

2. Cross out the numbers on the following list that are not prime numbers.

23	7	15	42	19	11
27	36	63	70	45	121

3. List all of the factors of the following numbers.

   a) 18   b) 24   c) 20   d) 33   e) 16   f) 30

4. Find the common factors of the following pairs of numbers.

   a) 8 and 12   b) 12 and 16   c) 12 and 18

   d) 18 and 27   e) 15 and 25   f) 20 and 30

5. List the first 6 multiples of the following numbers.

   a) 5   b) 10   c) 7   d) 4   e) 8   f) 11

6. True or false?

   a) 235 is a multiple of 5   b) 432 is a multiple of 6

   c) 619 is a multiple of 7   d) 567 is a multiple of 9

   e) 468 is a multiple of 8   f) 979 is a multiple of 11

Recap

- I can tell the difference between odd and even numbers.   ○ ○ ○

- I know what factors and products are.   ○ ○ ○

- I know what prime and composite numbers are.   ○ ○ ○

- I can find common factors of numbers.   ○ ○ ○

- I know what multiples are.   ○ ○ ○

5. Lines and Angles

Talk About

Lines

Have a look at the photograph of a railway track.
Can you find an example of each of these lines?

Horizontal line	Vertical line	Oblique line	Parallel lines	Perpendicular lines

1. Draw your own picture to illustrate these lines. Make sure to include them all.

2. Can you make up your own definitions for these lines?

    a) Parallel lines are lines that ...

    b) Perpendicular lines are lines that ...

Investigate drawing parallel and perpendicular lines using a ruler and a set square.

Look around the classroom and write down 6 examples of each type of line. Try to find unusual ones that others may not see, such as under your chair.

How would you check to see if the lines of your table or the whiteboard were level? Think of a few different things you could use to do this.

Strand: Shape and Space
Curriculum Objectives:
Recognise, classify and describe angles and relate angles to shape and the environment;
recognise angles in terms of a rotation;
estimate, measure and construct angles in degrees;
explore the sum of the angles in a triangle.

3. This is a photo of the GPO in Dublin. Examine and discuss the various lines you can see. Here are some phrases to help you:

The columns are _____ to the steps.

The _____ are parallel to each other.

4. Write down your full name using only capital letters. How many examples of horizontal, vertical, oblique, parallel and perpendicular lines can you find?

Puzzler

Can you work out what the mystery person's name is?
(Their name is written in block capitals.)

● The first letter is made up of 2 vertical parallel lines joined by a perpendicular line.

● The second letter is made up of 1 vertical line with 3 horizontal perpendicular lines.

● The third letter is made up of 1 vertical line with 1 horizontal perpendicular line.

● The fourth letter is the same as the second letter.

● The fifth and final letter is made up of 2 vertical parallel lines joined by 1 oblique line.

Angles

An **angle** is formed when 2 straight lines meet.

The size of the angle is the amount of space between the 2 lines.

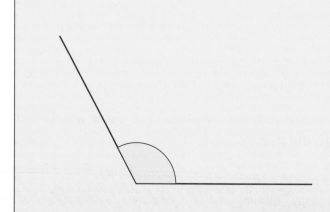

1. Match the angle with its correct name.

Right angle   **Acute angle**   **Obtuse angle**

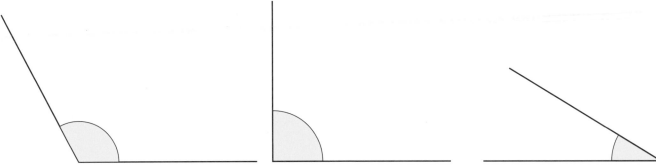

2. Can you complete these definitions of the angles you learned about last year?

   a) An acute angle is an angle that is _____ than a right angle.

   b) An obtuse angle is an angle that is _____ than a right angle.

Angle Assessment

3. a) How many right angles can you find on the surface of your table?

   b) If the door was slightly open, what angle would it make with the frame of the door?

   c) Name the angle that the legs of your chair make with the seat of the chair.

   d) Stretch out the fingers on 1 hand. What angle is being made between each finger?

   e) What angle is being made by your pen and the paper when you write?

   f) Count the number of right angles you can find on the whiteboard.

This is a straight line or **straight angle**.

How many right angles is it equal to?   _____

Find some examples of straight angles around you.

This is a **reflex angle**.

Is it greater than or less than a straight angle?

Investigate using straws or lollipop sticks.

First make a straight angle and then move 1 of the straws/sticks to make a reflex angle.

Is the angle getting bigger or smaller?

Find some examples of reflex angles around you.

> Construct a picture using straws or lollipop sticks. Name the angles used.
>
> An angle is a measure of **rotation** and is measured in degrees (°).
>
> A full rotation or full turn is 360 degrees, or 360°.

4. a) $\frac{1}{4}$ of a full turn (or $\frac{1}{4}$ of 360°) is a right angle and measures _____°.

   b) $\frac{1}{2}$ of a full turn (or $\frac{1}{2}$ of 360°) is a straight angle and measures _____°.

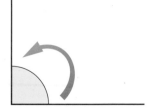

> You have just found that a right angle has 90° and a straight angle has 180°. You can now fill in the following.

5. a) An acute angle is _____ than a right angle and measures between 0° and _____°.

   b) An obtuse angle is _____ than a right angle and measures between 90° and _____°.

   c) A reflex angle is _____ than a straight angle and measures between 180° and _____°.

> Demonstrate these rotations on your table using 2 pencils. To make an acute angle, place both pencils beside each other to start. Hold 1 still and move the other to make a right angle. An acute angle can measure from the pencil you are holding still to a right angle (90°).

6. Draw and label an example of each of these angles.
   a) right angle
   b) acute angle
   c) obtuse angle
   d) straight angle
   e) reflex angle

7. Name each of the angles you can spot in these signs.

Find and draw some other road signs you know and mark all of the angles on each.

8. Have a look at the following clock faces. What angles are being made by the hands of each clock? Is there more than 1 angle being made?

a)

b)

c)

d)

e)

f)

9. Name the angle in each of the following (acute, right, obtuse, straight, reflex angle or full rotation).

a) 25°   b) 130°   c) 90°   d) 290°   e) 150°   f) 5°

g) 360°   h) 72°   i) 195°   j) 180°   k) 110°   l) 58°

10. Pick 5 of the angles in question 9 and draw what you think they might look like.

11. Use a clock to help you represent the following angles.

a) acute angle   b) right angle   c) obtuse angle   d) reflex angle

12. If there are 360° in a full rotation, 180° in a half rotation and 90° in a quarter rotation, through how many degrees does the hour hand on a clock turn, going clockwise, in the following? (Use a clock to help you or draw the times on clock faces.)

a) 12 o'clock to 3 o'clock   b) 3 o'clock to 9 o'clock

c) 1 o'clock to 7 o'clock   d) 12 o'clock to 12 o'clock

e) 9 o'clock to 12 o'clock   f) 5 o'clock to 8 o'clock

13. Calculate how many degrees are in each of the following.

a) $\frac{1}{4}$ of a full rotation   b) $\frac{1}{2}$ of a full rotation

c) $\frac{3}{4}$ of a full rotation   d) $\frac{1}{3}$ of a full rotation

e) $\frac{1}{12}$ of a full rotation   f) $\frac{1}{8}$ of a full rotation

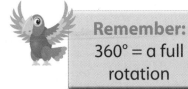

Remember:
360° = a full rotation

14. Draw clock faces with times to represent:

    a) $\frac{1}{4}$ of a full rotation

    b) $\frac{1}{2}$ of a full rotation

    c) $\frac{3}{4}$ of a full rotation

15. Decide whether each of the following angles are nearer to 90° or 180°.

    a)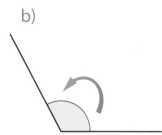

    b)

    c)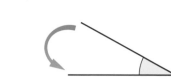

    d)

16. Estimate how many degrees are in each of these angles.

    a)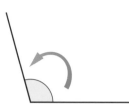

    b)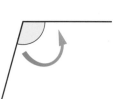

    c)

    d)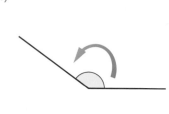

17. When would we need to get exact measurements of angles? Think of 3 examples.

When we want to measure angles, we use a protractor.

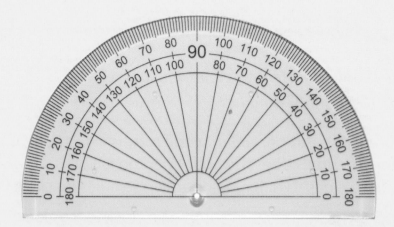

It has a baseline with a centre point and 2 marked scales from 0° to 180°.

Examine your protractor and discuss why it has 2 scales: 1 starting from the right of the protractor and 1 starting from the left.

When measuring an angle, remember to place the baseline of the protractor along 1 of the lines of the angle and the point of the angle on the centre point of the protractor.

18. Name these angles. Estimate the size of each and then check your estimate by measuring them with your protractor.

a)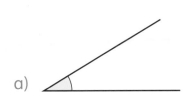

b)

c)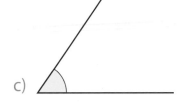

d)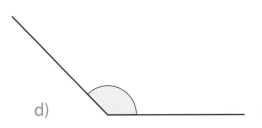

e)

f)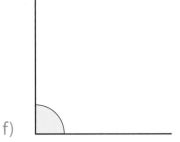

g)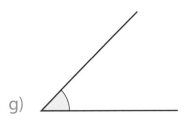

h)

19. Have a go at drawing these angles using only your ruler and pencil. When finished, check how accurate you are by measuring the angle with your protractor and write down the difference.

a) 20°	b) 170°	c) 90°	d) 45°
e) 100°	f) 10°	g) 135°	h) 70°

20. Draw these angles using a pencil, ruler and protractor.

a) 80°	b) 120°	c) 95°	d) 5°
e) 60°	f) 140°	g) 15°	h) 165°
i) 180°	j) 30°	k) 110°	l) 22°

When drawing angles, **remember:**
- Draw 1 line of the angle with a ruler.
- Place the baseline of the protractor on this line, with the centre point on the end of the line.
- Follow the scale to the angle you want and mark this point.
- Join this point to the end of your line.

21. Look around the classroom. Find 5 angles and estimate their size. Check your answer by measuring the angle with your protractor.

22. How many degrees are in each angle?
    (Hint: for e) and f), things might go upside down!)

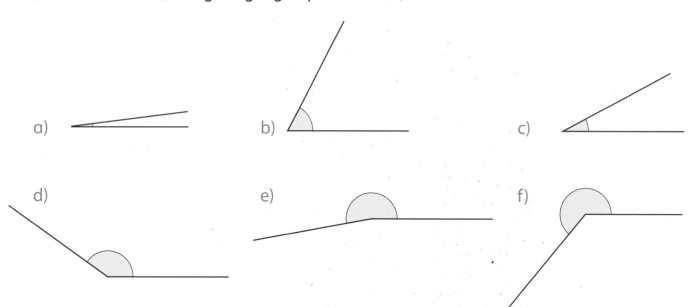

a)   b)   c)

d)   e)   f)

23. How many angles can you locate in this picture? Estimate the size of each and then check your guess using your protractor.

24. If a right angle = 90° and a straight angle = 180°, find the missing angle in each of these.

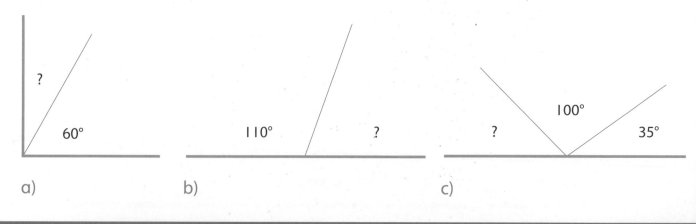

?   60°   110°   ?   ?   100°   35°

a)   b)   c)

25. Draw a triangle on a piece of paper using a ruler. Cut out the triangle and mark the 3 angles. Tear off the 3 angles and fit them together. What angle do they make when fitted together?

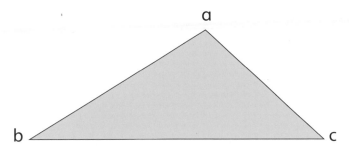

26. Measure each of the above angles accurately with your protractor and add the 3 angles together.

   a) angle a = _____   b) angle b = _____   c) angle c = _____

   d) angle a + angle b + angle c = _____

27. Cut out 2 more different types of triangle and investigate what the angles add up to. Now complete this sentence:

   The 3 angles of a triangle add up to a _____ angle or _____°.

28. Using your results from question 27, can you find the measurement of the missing angles in each of these triangles?

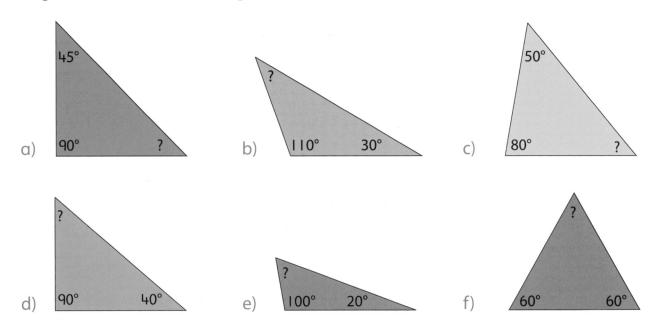

a) 45° 90° ?   b) ? 110° 30°   c) 50° 80° ?

d) ? 90° 40°   e) ? 100° 20°   f) ? 60° 60°

29. Make a set of instructions to take you from your seat in the classroom to the door, blackboard or teacher's table. Include as many direction changes as possible.

30. Write a set of instructions for someone to walk in the shape of the following.
   a) square   b) rectangle   c) triangle

Tangrams

1. Examine your tangrams and name all of the angles you can see.

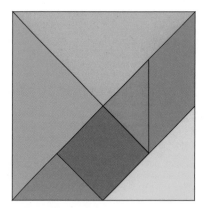

2. Make the following shapes using your tangram pieces. Can you name all of the angles in each shape?

a) b) c)

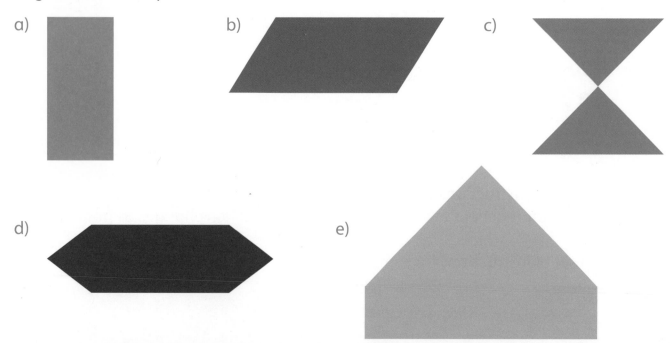

d) e)

Homework

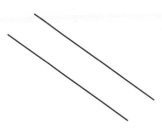

1. Identify these lines by writing the right name beside each.

   a)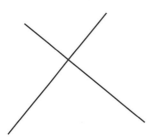

   b)

   c)

   d)

   e)

2. Are the following angles acute, obtuse, reflex, straight or right?

   a)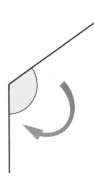

   b)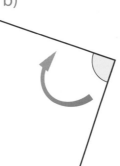

   c)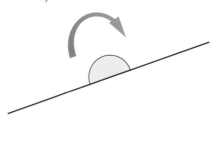

   d)

   e)

3. Name the angle: acute, right, obtuse, straight, reflex or full rotation.

   a) 143°   b) 79°   c) 180°   d) 300°

   e) 360°   f) 90°   g) 195°   h) 175°

4. Estimate the size of each of these angles. Check your estimate by measuring them with your protractor.

a)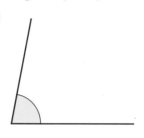

b)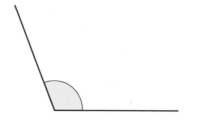

c)

d)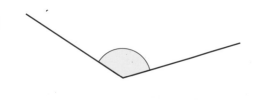

e)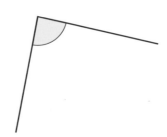

5. Draw these angles using a pencil, ruler and protractor.

When drawing angles, **remember:**
- Draw 1 line of the angle with a ruler.
- Place the baseline of the protractor on this line, with the centre point on the end of the line.
- Follow the scale to the angle you want and mark this point.
- Join this point to the end of your line.

a) 50°   b) 160°   c) 85°   d) 25°
e) 70°   f) 135°   g) 40°   h) 115°

6. Work out the missing angles in each of these triangles.

a)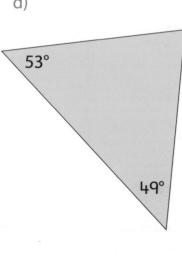

b)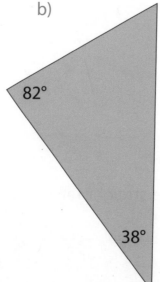

c)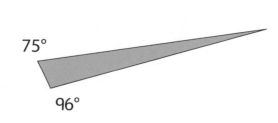

- I can recognise and classify types of line. ○ ○ ○

- I can recognise and classify types of angle. ○ ○ ○

- I can estimate and measure angles. ○ ○ ○

- I can construct angles. ○ ○ ○

6. Equations

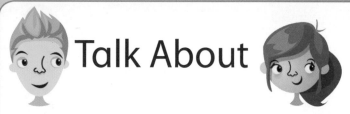

Talk About

Make Number Sentences Out of Word Problems

Complete these language sentences.

My name is _____ and I live in _____.

My dream for the future is to _____.

Now look at how we can change this language sentence into a number sentence:
I am ten years old and in three years I will be thirteen.

$$10 + 3 = 13$$

A number sentence contains numbers and symbols.

1. Change these into number sentences.

    a) I am _____ years old, but five years ago I was _____. (_____ − 5 = _____)

    b) I am _____ years old and if you double my age the answer is _____.

    Can you write 2 different number sentences for this one?

    c) I am _____ metres tall. The difference in height between myself and the person beside me is _____.

    d) The time now is _____ and in 20 minutes it will be _____.

    e) Think up 3 of your own sentences and convert them to number sentences.

2. Here are some number sentences. The frame _____ is the part we don't know.
   Fill in the frames using the appropriate numbers or symbols (+ − × ÷ =).

    a) 150 + 45 = _____   b) 36 _____ 19 = 17   c) 57 + _____ = 90

    d) 12 × 3 = _____   e) _____ − 10 = 66   f) 5 _____ 40 ÷ 8

    g) 28 + _____ = 110   h) 2 × _____ = 112   i) 1450 _____ 10 = 145

Strand: Algebra
Curriculum Objectives:
Translate number sentences with a frame into word problems and vice versa;
solve one-step number sentences and equations.

3. Now try these.

   a) $6.5 - 1.5 =$ _____

   b) $\frac{1}{2} + \frac{1}{4} =$ _____

   c) $\frac{1}{2}$ of _____ $= 10$

   d) $\frac{1}{3}$ of $150 =$ _____

   e) 7.32 _____ $4.67 = 2.65$

   f) $0.2 + 1.9 =$ _____

   g) $60 \div$ _____ $= 20$

   h) 12 _____ $3 = 36$

   i) $11{:}45am - 15$ mins $=$ _____

4. Just as with language sentences, number sentences may not always be true. For each of the following, say whether each number statement is true or false.

   a) $345 + 68 = 403$

   b) $\frac{1}{4}$ of $96 = 24$

   c) $9 \times 8 = 72$

   d) $95 > 115$

   e) $16 = 240 \div 12$

   f) $1896 - 652 = 1132$

   g) Correct any false statements.

   h) Create a few statements of your own.

5. Here is a class photograph of 30 children. Change the following sentences to number sentences and find the answers.

   a) The teacher would like to organise the classroom into groups seating 6 children. How many groups can she have? ($30 \div 6 =$ _____)

   b) This afternoon, 6 children are going to a table quiz final. How many will be left in the classroom then?

   c) The teacher decides to have a table quiz with the remaining children in the class. She organises 6 equal teams. How many children are in each team?

   d) The next day, all 30 children are completing art projects. They are all either painting or sketching. If 13 children are painting, how many are sketching?

   e) Make up 2 more questions based on this class. Ask the person next to you to solve them.

6. In the following tables, can you figure out the number sentences and fill in the gaps? For example, in table A: $1 \times \underline{\quad} = 3, 2 \times \underline{\quad} = 6$

A

×	
1	3
2	6
3	
4	12
5	
6	

B

−	
100	89
90	
80	69
70	
60	
50	39

C

÷	
10	2
20	
30	
40	8
50	10
60	

7. Karen thought of a number, subtracted 27 from it and was left with 62. What was the number?

8. Lee thought of a number, divided it by 8 and his answer was 65. What was the number?

9. Anne had 47 cards after her friend gave her 13 cards. How many had she at first?

Make Word Problems from Number Sentences

1. Invent stories for the following number sentences.

   a) $72 - 12 = \underline{\quad}$ (e.g. Dylan had 72 marbles but lost 12 of them in a game. How many has he left?)

   b) $21 + 7 = \underline{\quad}$
   c) $9 \times 14 = \underline{\quad}$
   d) $\underline{\quad} - 10 = 139$

   e) $81 \div \underline{\quad} = 9$
   f) $\underline{\quad} \times 6 = 66$
   g) $\underline{\quad} + 2 = 31$

Solve Equations

A number sentence with an equal sign (=) is called an **equation**.

We must equate or equalise the numbers on both sides of the equal sign.

For example, $5 + 9 = \underline{\quad}$.

To solve this, we simply add the numbers, giving the answer 14.

1. Have a go at solving these equations.

a) $39 + 42 =$ _____

b) $195 - 78 =$ _____

c) $5 \times 11 =$ _____

d) $64 \div 4 =$ _____

e) $9 = 72 \div$ _____

f) $230 +$ _____ $= 346$

g) _____ $- 44 = 135$

h) $8 \times$ _____ $= 112$

Write questions 2 to 5 as equations and work out the answers.

2. James had some sweets. He ate 7 and had 12 left. How many had he at first?

$$\text{\_\_\_\_\_} - 7 = 12$$

3. Tom had €40 and bought a pair of jeans for €22.50.
   How much money did he have left?

4. If a television programme lasts 45 minutes and started at
   6:30pm, at what time will it finish?

5. Ailbhe bought 4 pens at 50c each. How much did she spend?

6. Complete these equations using your calculator.

a) $6980 + 2349 =$ _____

b) $10455 - 6599 =$ _____

c) $298 \times 16 =$ _____

d) $6480 \div 12 =$ _____

e) $\frac{1}{3}$ of $561 =$ _____

f) $1978 +$ _____ $= 2564$

g) _____ $\times 9 = 14121$

h) $25150 \div$ _____ $= 5030$

i) $9.34 - 2.56 =$ _____

j) _____ $\times 92 = 55936$

Puzzler

By adding one thing, how can you make this equation correct?

10   10   10 = 9.50

You may have to think outside the box for this one!

World Cup Basketball

	American All Stars	German Giants
1st quarter	14 points	12 points
2nd quarter	18 points	21 points
3rd quarter	22 points	16 points
4th quarter	10 points	18 points

7. It's the World Cup Basketball final and the commentators need your help working out some statistics of the match. Change each of the following to equations and work out the answers for them.

   a) Each basket scored in the 1st quarter was worth 2 points. How many baskets did each team score?

   b) The total points for a team is found by adding the points won from each quarter. What was the score for both teams after the 2nd quarter?

   c) Amazing Andy from the All Stars scored 15 baskets of 2 points each. How many points did he score altogether?

   d) What was the difference between the teams, in points, in the 3rd quarter?

   e) Who won the match?

8. Devise a few of your own stories for these.

   a) $61 + 32 =$ _____

   b) $39 \div$ _____ $= 13$

   c) $540 -$ _____ $= 80$

   d) $24 \times 5 =$ _____

   e) _____ $+ 120 = 710$

   f) $96 \div 8 =$ _____

   g) $10\text{:}25\text{am} + 1 \text{ hr } 20 \text{ mins} =$ _____

   h) $\frac{1}{6}$ of $114 =$ _____

   i) $1\text{kg } 130\text{g} -$ _____ $= 500\text{g}$

Puzzle Squares

1. a) Addition:
       All horizontal, vertical and oblique lines add up to 15.

   b) Multiplication

   c) Multiplication:
       Find the numbers to multiply by.

a)

6		8
	5	
2		

b)

×	4	11	6
9			
7			
12			

c)

×			
	49	56	21
	28	32	12
	63	72	27

1. Complete these number sentences by filling in the missing symbol (+, −, ×, ÷).

   a) 67 ___ 78 = 145

   b) 28 ___ 17 = 476

   c) 163 ___ 89 = 74

   d) 192 ___ 8 = 24

   e) 204 ___ 186 = 18

   f) 177 ___ 3 = 59

Make the word problems in questions 2 to 5 into number sentences and then solve them.

2. Joe spent €38.99 on a new pair of runners. If he paid with a €50 note, how much change did he receive?

3. In her stamp collection, Karen has 47 stamps from India, 39 stamps from Bangladesh and 26 stamps from Pakistan. How many stamps does she have in her collection altogether?

4. If every packet of sweets contains 8 sweets and there are 608 sweets altogether, how many full packets of sweets can be made?

5. There are 16 teams in the league and 14 players in each team's squad. How many players are participating in the league altogether?

6. Use your calculator to solve these equations.

   a) $\frac{1}{9}$ of 9756 = _____

   b) 2589 + _____ = 8410

   c) _____ × 24 = 4728

   d) 7324 ÷ _____ = 1831

   e) 7.2 − 4.56 = _____

   f) 23451 + 8629 = _____

   g) 564 × 38 = _____

   h) 20% of _____ = 238

7. Make up word problems for the following number sentences.

   a) 23 × 7 = _____

   b) 96 ÷ 4 = _____

   c) 298 + 356 + 402 = _____

   d) 4380 − 1978 = _____

Recap

- I can make number sentences out of word problems. ○ ○ ○

- I can make up word problems from number sentences. ○ ○ ○

- I can solve equations. ○ ○ ○

7. Time

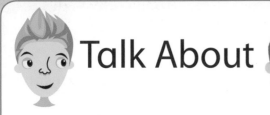  ## Talk About

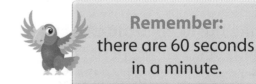

Remember:
there are 60 seconds
in a minute.

Banana Bonanza

Contestants in a game show were awarded 1 point for every second that they managed to balance a banana on their nose. If a man kept the banana on his nose for 1 minute and 24 seconds, how many points did he get?

1 minute 24 seconds = 60 + 24 seconds
= 84 seconds = 84 points

1. How many points did these contestants get?

   a) 1 min 37 sec   b) 1 min 53 sec   c) 2 min 18 sec   d) 2 min 35 sec

   e) 3 min 20 sec   f) 4 min 5 sec   g) 6 min 42 sec   h) 9 min 17 sec

2. If the following contestants scored these points, work out in minutes and seconds how long they managed to balance the banana on their nose.

   a) 68 points   b) 85 points   c) 103 points   d) 192 points

   e) 157 points   f) 208 points   g) 289 points   h) 417 points

3. The next game required the contestants to juggle 4 bananas while whistling the national anthem over and over again. For every full minute they managed to do this, they were awarded 2 points. How many points did these contestants get?

   a) 38 minutes   b) 1 hr 10 mins   c) 1 hr 47 mins   d) 1 hr 58 mins

   e) 2 hrs   f) 2 hrs 30 mins   g) 2 hrs 51 mins   h) 3 hrs 34 mins

4. How long in hours and minutes did these contestants last?

   a) 114 points = _____ minutes = _____ hours _____ minutes

   b) 144 points   c) 186 points   d) 204 points   e) 268 points

   f) 310 points   g) 378 points   h) 422 points   i) 444 points

Strand: Measures
Curriculum Objectives:
Read and interpret timetables and the 24-hour clock (digital and analogue);
interpret and convert between times in 12-hour and 24-hour format.

 54

Change Times from the 12-hour to the 24-hour Clock

If there are 24 hours in a day, how come most clocks only go as far as 12?

If you lived in northern Norway, where there are 24 hours of constant daylight for a time during the summer and 24 hours of constant darkness for a time during the winter, how could a 12-hour clock be potentially confusing?

How might this confusion be avoided?

AM

PM

When we use the 24-hour clock system to mark time, the day starts at 00:00 hours (which is midnight) and moves to 23:59 before moving back to 00:00 hours. 12:00 hours is midday, or noon. When we use the 24-hour clock we have no use for am or pm. **All times on the 24-hour clock are written with 4 digits.**

am to 24 Hour	pm to 24 Hour
12:14am = 00:14 hours	12:25pm = 12:25 hours
6:42am = 06:42 hours	7:19pm = 19:19 hours
10:30am = 10:30 hours	11:56pm = 23:56 hours

What do you notice about the times and how they change? Can you see any patterns? Discuss it with the people near you.

1. Now see if you can write these times in the 24-hour system. (Remember to use 4 digits.)

    a) 9:02am   b) 11:15am   c) 3:45pm   d) 12:26am

    e) 6:01pm   f) 8:53pm   g) 2:35am   h) 10:18pm

2. Now try it the opposite way. Remember to identify the times as am or pm.

    a) 13:00   b) 05:40   c) 21:25   d) 00:30

    e) 12:20   f) 16:55   g) 11:05   h) 09:35

Adding Times

1. Tom fell asleep when the time on his clock read 7:35. If he was asleep for 1 hour 40 minutes, work out in your head what time was on the clock when he woke up.

7:35 + 1:40 =   7:35 + 1:00 = 8:35   8:35 + 0:25 = 9:00

Now just work out how many minutes are left to add on to get the correct time.

2. Work these times out in your head.

    a) 1:55 + 1:10   b) 2:45 + 1:30   c) 3:35 + 2:45

    d) 1:20 + 2:55   e) 2:15 + 3:50   f) 5:55 + 4:25

Cinemagic

3. a) Work out what time each film ended.

    b) Write the starting time and the finishing time of each film in the 24-hour system.

    c) If the cinema put on *The Secret Room* again at 11:50pm, at what time would it finish?

    d) If an earlier show of *Supercat* finished at 8:54pm, at what time did it start?

Screen	Film	Starting Time	Duration
1	*The Secret Room*	8:15pm	2 hrs 28 mins
2	*Attack of the Deadly Carrots*	7:55pm	2 hrs 17 mins
3	*Supercat*	9:25pm	1 hr 49 mins
4	*Sleepwalkers*	11:40pm	1 hr 57 mins

Puzzler

Susan, Jane and Kevin work in different shops in the shopping centre. Susan gets a break every 120 minutes, Jane gets a break every 180 minutes and Kevin gets a break every 360 minutes. If they each work from 9:00am to 5:00pm, will they all have a break at the same time? If yes, at what time?

4. Now try these.

a)
hrs	mins
1	27
+ 2	38

b)
hrs	mins
4	39
+ 1	26

c)
hrs	mins
2	13
+ 4	57

d)
hrs	mins
5	46
+ 2	56

e)
hrs	mins
2	19
1	36
+ 3	24

f)
hrs	mins
1	45
3	27
+ 1	18

g)
hrs	mins
3	28
2	49
+ 4	55

h)
hrs	mins
4	53
1	37
+ 6	47

5. If a man worked for 3 hours 48 minutes in the morning and 2 hours 39 minutes in the afternoon, for how long was he working altogether?

6. In a competition, Sarah managed to balance on a basketball while juggling 3 remote controls for 1 hour 36 minutes. Her friend Tara managed to do it for 49 minutes longer than Sarah. What was Tara's overall time?

Subtracting Times

Jack took 1 hour 15 minutes to do his homework. It took Jill 20 minutes less. Work out in your head how long it took Jill to do her homework.

If **1:15 – 0:15 = 1:00**, then **1:15 – 0:20 = 55 minutes**

1. Now try these in your head.

    a) 1:05 – 0:25　　　　b) 1:35 – 0:50　　　　c) 2:15 – 1:35

    d) 2:20 – 0:55　　　　e) 3:25 – 1:40　　　　f) 4:50 – 0:55

If Jane went to see a film that was 2 hours 12 minutes long but she fell asleep for 28 minutes, how much of the film did she actually see?

	hrs	mins
	2	12
–		28

You can't take 28 minutes from 12 minutes because there are not enough minutes on top, but you can borrow 1 hour from the 2 hours that you have.

	hrs	mins
	$\overset{1}{\cancel{2}}$	$\overset{72}{\cancel{12}}$
–	1	28
	1	44

Remember: 1 hour = 60 minutes

2. Now try these.

    a)
	hrs	mins
	2	47
–	1	38

    b)
	hrs	mins
	4	19
–	1	46

    c)
	hrs	mins
	4	23
–	3	57

    d)
	hrs	mins
	5	36
–	2	51

    e)
	hrs	mins
	8	25
–	5	54

    f)
	hrs	mins
	6	37
–	4	49

    g)
	hrs	mins
	9	04
–	7	18

    h)
	hrs	mins
	10	12
–	9	36

Reading a Timetable

Bus Timetable

Journey	Departure Time	Arrival Time
Cork to Galway	9:15am	12:45pm
Dublin to Limerick	1:30pm	4:10pm
Belfast to Sligo	11:25am	2:38pm
Athlone to Tralee	10:40pm	1:15am

1. Change this timetable so that all the times are recorded in the 24-hour system. Draw it into your copy.

   a) If the bus to Galway is delayed by 37 minutes, at what time will it reach its destination? Remember: there are only 60 minutes in 1 hour.

   b) If the bus to Limerick is 28 minutes early, at what time will it reach its destination?

   c) Work out how much time it takes for each of the journeys.

   d) Which was the longest journey and which was the shortest journey in terms of time?

   e) How much longer was the longest journey compared to the shortest journey?

Work Out the Difference between Times

2. Based on your work for question 1 above, can you suggest any tips or rules about finding the difference between 2 times? Discuss this with the people around you.

3. Find the difference between these times. Remember to change them to the 24-hour system before subtracting.

   a) 9:17am and 11:45am
   b) 7:42pm and 10:23pm
   c) 11:36am and 1:54pm
   d) 7:49am and 5:21pm
   e) 6:47pm and 9:03pm
   f) 10:39am and 3:16pm
   g) 2:51am and 10:27pm
   h) 5:11pm and 11:04pm

What's on TV?

CTV 1	Films 24
17:30 *The Magic of Magic*	16:30 *The Last Boat from Luxor*
18:00 *Who Shot Lassie?*	18:05 *Cats Go Crazy*
18:45 *Cartoon Chaos*	19:55 *The Time Sentinels*
19:05 *Gardening Weekly*	22:15 *Journey to the Stars*
19:40 *Who Will Buy Your House?*	00:00 *The Luminous Ones*
20:25 *Tall Tales*	01:35 *Gridlock 5*
21:00 *News Headlines*	03:30 *The House That Time Forgot*
21:13 *Weather Report*	05:45 *Closedown*
21:20 *Heavenly Holidays*	

4. Write the starting times of the following programmes in am or pm (refer to the schedule on the previous page).

   a) *The Last Boat from Luxor*   b) *Cartoon Chaos*

   c) *Tall Tales*   d) *Gridlock 5*

5. How long is each of the following programmes?

   a) *Cartoon Chaos*   b) *Journey to the Stars*

   c) *Who Will Buy Your House?*   d) *The Time Sentinels*

6. If you only watched the following sets of programmes, for how long would you have been watching television?

   a) *Who Shot Lassie?* and *The Time Sentinels*

   b) *Gardening Weekly* and *Gridlock 5*

   c) *Who Will Buy Your House?* and *The Luminous Ones*

   d) *The House That Time Forgot* and *Weather Report* and *Cats Go Crazy*

7. If you started watching the film *The Time Sentinels* but then switched over to CTV1 to watch *Tall Tales*, *News Headlines* and *Weather Report* before switching back to see the end of the film, how much of the film would you have seen?

8. Why is Film 24 an inappropriate name for that TV station?

Homework

1. How many seconds are in each of the following?

   a) 1 min 26 sec   b) 3 mins 15 sec   c) 2 mins 47 sec   d) 5 mins 31 sec

   e) 4 mins 7 sec   f) 9 mins 52 sec   g) 6 mins 11 sec   h) 10 mins 40 sec

2. How many minutes are in each of the following?

   a) 1 hr 38 mins   b) 1 hr 58 mins   c) 3 hrs 22 mins   d) 4 hrs 29 mins

   e) 2 hrs 26 mins   f) 7 hrs 10 mins   g) 5 hrs 9 mins   h) 8 hrs 44 mins

3. Now try these.

a)	hrs	mins		b)	hrs	mins		c)	hrs	mins		d)	hrs	mins
	3	52			4	17			2	25			3	30
+	1	19		+	2	09		+	1	48		+	2	53

e)	hrs	mins	f)	hrs	mins	g)	hrs	mins	h)	hrs	mins
	1	32		2	27		4	34		5	29
	1	18		1	56		4	10		2	38
+	1	42	+	2	08	+	1	47	+	3	19

i)	hrs	mins	j)	hrs	mins	k)	hrs	mins	l)	hrs	mins
	3	28		2	22		8	30		6	16
−	1	09	−	1	37	−	4	44	−	2	27

m)	hrs	mins	n)	hrs	mins	o)	hrs	mins	p)	hrs	mins
	8	07		9	51		7	45		10	40
−	1	23	−	4	54	−	7	19	−	6	43

4. Here is an extract from Ms Numberlover's timetable for her 5th class.

Time	Monday	Time	Monday
09:00	English	12:35	Lunch
09:45	Gaeilge	13:05	PE
10:30	Break	14:00	Science
10:45	Maths	14:35	Home
12:00	Music		

a) How long did Ms Numberlover allow for Gaeilge?

b) To what activity did she devote the most time?

c) What was the combined time spent on Music and PE?

d) How much longer did the class spend on English than Science?

e) What is the total combined recreation time?

f) How long, in total, were the children in class?

Recap

- I can change times from the 12-hour to the 24-hour clock.

- I can add times.

- I can take one time away from another.

- I can read a timetable.

- I can use a timetable to work out the difference between times.

8. Fractions I

Talk About

Puzzler

The hungry twins, Horace and Hector, were invited to their friend Helen's birthday party. Horace was particularly hungry that day and he ate 8 slices of pizza. Hector, on the other hand, decided that he would only have 5 slices, as he did not want to appear greedy. Helen, however, pointed out that both twins had eaten exactly the same amount of pizza. How could this be true?

1. Have you ever eaten a fraction?
2. Have you ever drunk a fraction?
3. If you met an alien, how would describe to it what a fraction is?
4. What is the bottom number of a fraction called?
5. What does it tell us?
6. What is the top number of a fraction called?
7. What does it tell us?
8. The red portion is the amount of pizza that the children ate at a party.

Tim

Tina

Lisa

David

Mary

Conor

Jamie

Peter

a) Who ate the most amount of pizza?
b) Who ate the least amount of pizza?
c) Which 2 people ate the same amount of pizza?
d) What can we say about the fractions that those 2 people ate?

Strand: Number
Curriculum Objectives:
Compare and order fractions and identify equivalent forms of fractions with denominators 2–12.

A fraction is written in a very particular way. If you're still thinking about pizza, then $\frac{5}{6}$ of a pizza is a pizza that has been divided into 6 equal slices and has had 1 slice taken away.

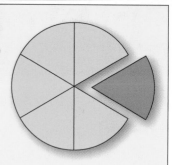

$$\frac{\text{numerator}}{\text{denominator}} \qquad \frac{5}{6} \qquad \frac{\text{number of sixths}}{\text{family of fractions (sixths)}}$$

Different fractions that are equal to the same amount are called **equivalent fractions**.

This fraction wall shows us how fractions can be equivalent.

$\frac{1}{2}$ is the same as $\frac{2}{4}$ or $\frac{3}{6}$ or $\frac{4}{8}$ or $\frac{6}{12}$.

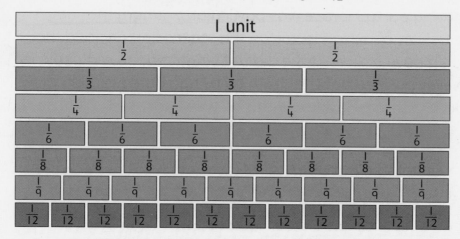

If Lisa has $\frac{3}{4}$ of her pizza left and Tom has $\frac{9}{12}$ of his left, who has more pizza left?

What can we say about $\frac{3}{4}$ and $\frac{9}{12}$?

$\frac{3}{4}$ and $\frac{9}{12}$ are equivalent fractions.

This pizza has been divided into 8 slices. If you eat all 8 slices, what fraction of the pizza have you eaten?

8 slices $= \frac{8}{8} = 1$ whole pizza

Remember: when the numerator and the denominator are the same, then the fraction is equal to 1, or 1 whole.

We call fractions like these members of the family of 1.

1. Solve these very difficult multiplication questions!

    a) 7×1

    b) 9×1

    c) 5×1

    d) 10×1

    e) 12×1

    f) 47×1

What do you notice about the answers? So $\frac{3}{4} \times 1 =$ _____

$$\frac{3}{4} \times \frac{2}{2} = \frac{6}{8}$$

But if $\frac{2}{2} = 1$, then what can we say about $\frac{3}{4}$ and the answer?

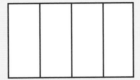 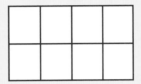

Shade the amount represented by each fraction in order to check your answer.

2. Now try these. Draw your own boxes and shade them to check if your first fraction and your answer are equivalent (the same value).

    a) $\frac{1}{2} \times \frac{4}{4} =$

    b) $\frac{1}{4} \times \frac{3}{3} =$

    c) $\frac{1}{3} \times \frac{2}{2} =$

    d) $\frac{1}{6} \times \frac{2}{2} =$

    e) $\frac{2}{5} \times \frac{3}{3} =$

    f) $\frac{2}{3} \times \frac{4}{4} =$

3. Now try these equally hard division questions.

    a) $9 \div 1$

    b) $4 \div 1$

    c) $7 \div 1$

    d) $3 \div 1$

    e) $12 \div 1$

    f) $8 \div 1$

Again, what do you notice about the answers?

If we divide a fraction by a member of the family of 1, we will get an equivalent fraction.

Check this one to see if it's true.

$$\frac{6}{8} \div \frac{2}{2} =$$ _____

Is $\frac{6}{8}$ the same value (or amount of pizza) as your answer? How could you check it?

4. Find equivalent fractions for these by dividing.

a) $\dfrac{2}{4} \div \dfrac{2}{2} =$

b) $\dfrac{4}{8} \div \dfrac{5}{5} =$

c) $\dfrac{7}{21} \div \dfrac{7}{7} =$

d) $\dfrac{3}{9} \div \dfrac{3}{3} =$

e) $\dfrac{5}{25} \div \dfrac{5}{5} =$

f) $\dfrac{16}{24} \div \dfrac{8}{8} =$

g) $\dfrac{9}{12} \div \dfrac{3}{3} =$

h) $\dfrac{16}{20} \div \dfrac{4}{4} =$

i) $\dfrac{18}{45} \div \dfrac{9}{9} =$

What happens when you try this one?

$$\dfrac{5}{10} \div \dfrac{3}{3} = \underline{\hspace{2cm}}$$

Why can it not be done?

You have to find a number that divides equally into both 5 and 10.

We can divide only by a **factor** that is **common** to the numerator and the denominator (in other words, a number that divides equally into both).

By what member of the family of 1 could you have divided?
(Hint: can you think of a factor common to 5 and 10?)

What member of the family of 1 can you divide into $\frac{6}{10}$ to make an equivalent fraction?

$$\dfrac{6}{10} \div \dfrac{?}{?} = \underline{\hspace{2cm}}$$

You must find a factor that is common to both 6 and 10. Write out the list of their factors to help you.

$6 = 1, \underline{\hspace{0.8cm}}, \underline{\hspace{0.8cm}}, \underline{\hspace{0.8cm}}$

$10 = 1, \underline{\hspace{0.8cm}}, \underline{\hspace{0.8cm}}, \underline{\hspace{0.8cm}}$

Now you can divide.

---

5. Find equivalent fractions for these fractions by dividing by a member of the family of 1. (Remember to find a common factor first.)

a) $\dfrac{2}{8}$

b) $\dfrac{4}{10}$

c) $\dfrac{8}{10}$

d) $\dfrac{5}{15}$

Homework

1. Try these. Check that your answers are equivalent to the original fractions.

   a) $\dfrac{1}{4} \times \dfrac{2}{2} =$

   b) $\dfrac{2}{3} \times \dfrac{3}{3} =$

   c) $\dfrac{1}{5} \times \dfrac{4}{4} =$

   d) $\dfrac{3}{4} \times \dfrac{3}{3} =$

   e) $\dfrac{1}{2} \times \dfrac{5}{5} =$

   f) $\dfrac{3}{5} \times \dfrac{2}{2} =$

2. Now find equivalent fractions for the following fractions by multiplying by a member of the family of 1.

   a) $\dfrac{4}{5}$

   b) $\dfrac{1}{6}$

   c) $\dfrac{3}{4}$

   d) $\dfrac{5}{8}$

   e) $\dfrac{3}{10}$

   f) $\dfrac{2}{7}$

   g) $\dfrac{5}{9}$

   h) $\dfrac{7}{10}$

3. Try these. Check that your answers are equivalent to the original fractions.

   a) $\dfrac{3}{6} \div \dfrac{3}{3} =$

   b) $\dfrac{8}{12} \div \dfrac{4}{4} =$

   c) $\dfrac{6}{8} \div \dfrac{2}{2} =$

   d) $\dfrac{6}{9} \div \dfrac{3}{3} =$

   e) $\dfrac{15}{25} \div \dfrac{5}{5} =$

   f) $\dfrac{24}{32} \div \dfrac{8}{8} =$

   g) $\dfrac{14}{21} \div \dfrac{7}{7} =$

   h) $\dfrac{30}{36} \div \dfrac{6}{6} =$

   i) $\dfrac{27}{63} \div \dfrac{9}{9} =$

4. Now find equivalent fractions for the following fractions by dividing by a member of the family of 1.

   a) $\dfrac{18}{21}$

   b) $\dfrac{16}{28}$

   c) $\dfrac{15}{20}$

   d) $\dfrac{24}{64}$

   e) $\dfrac{35}{42}$

   f) $\dfrac{30}{40}$

   g) $\dfrac{9}{54}$

   h) $\dfrac{24}{30}$

Recap

- I know what equivalent fractions are.   ○ ○ ○
- I know how to make equivalent fractions.   ○ ○ ○

10. 2-D Shapes

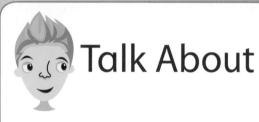 Talk About

2-D Shapes

1. Name these 2-D shapes.

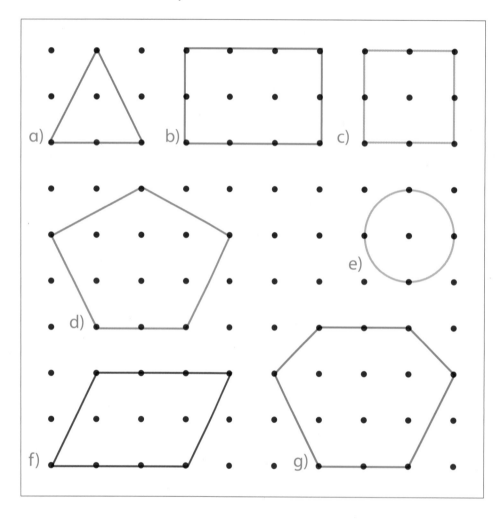

a)
b)
c)
d)
e)
f)
g)

If possible, make these shapes on a geoboard. Describe these shapes using the following headings: number of lines, number of angles, parallel lines and right angles.

2. Draw a picture using all of the shapes.

> These **two-dimensional (2-D) shapes** are so called because they have only 2 dimensions: length and width.

Strand: Shape and Space
Curriculum Objectives:
Make informal deductions about 2-D shapes and their properties; use angle and line properties to classify and describe triangles and quadrilaterals; tessellate combinations of 2-D shapes;

classify 2-D shapes according to their lines of symmetry; use 2-D shapes and properties to solve problems.

3. What shape am I? Choose the right shape from the list below.

> rectangle, square, octagon, triangle, isosceles triangle, pentagon

a) I have 3 sides.

b) I have as many sides as an octopus has legs.

c) I have 4 sides, each side of equal length.

d) I have 3 sides, 2 of which are the same length.

e) I have as many sides as you have toes on 1 foot.

f) I have 4 sides. The parallel sides are the same length.

Polygons

> 2-D shapes that have the same number of sides and angles are called **polygons**.

1. Make each of these polygons on a geoboard or with lollipop sticks and record how many sides and angles are in each one.

a) Triangle

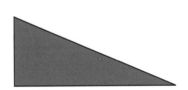

Sides: _____
Angles: _____

b) Octagon

Sides: _____
Angles: _____

c) Rhombus

Sides: _____
Angles: _____

d) Hexagon

Sides: _____
Angles: _____

e) Square

Sides: _____
Angles: _____

f) Quadrilateral

Sides: _____
Angles: _____

> A **regular polygon** is a polygon with sides of the same length and with angles that are all the same.

2. Here are 2 examples of regular polygons. What are they called? How many sides and angles do they have?

3. Try to draw some others into your copy: equilateral triangle, square, octagon.

Puzzler

A square is always a rectangle, but a rectangle is not always a square.

Is this statement true? Discuss it with the people near you. Decide whether it's true or not and what your reasons are for your decision.

When you get to the bottom of it, try it out on your parents at home to see if you can confuse them.

4. Write down a list of 6 regular polygons and find an example of each, either around the school or in your local area. Record them in a table like this:

	Regular Polygon	Example
1	Square	Floor tile
2		
3		
4		
5		
6		

Triangles

There are 3 types of triangle that you have met before.

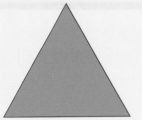

Equilateral triangle

Isosceles triangle

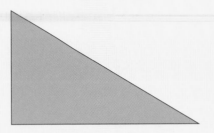

Scalene triangle

Each triangle is different, depending on the number of sides of equal length it has and on the number of equal angles.

1. So now you can fill in the gaps.

    a) Equilateral triangle

    _____ equal sides

    _____ equal angles

    of ____°

    b) Isosceles triangle

    _____ equal sides

    _____ equal angles

    c) Scalene triangle

    _____ equal sides

    _____ equal angles

    | Each of these triangles is equilateral, isosceles or scalene, but which is which? Can you tell? |

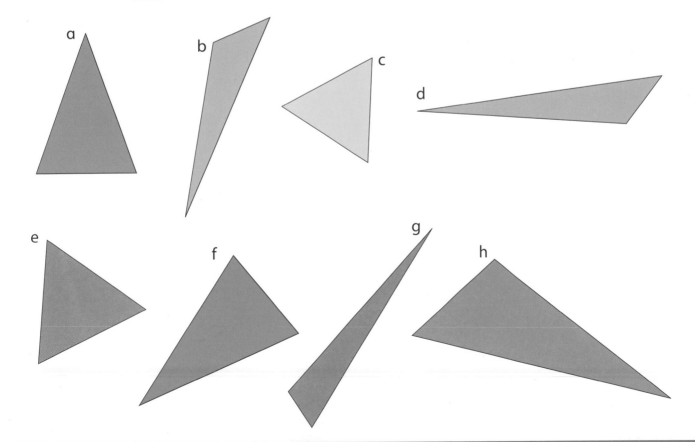

Puzzler

Draw and cut out an equilateral and isosceles triangle.
Which one can you then divide into 4 equal triangles?

Quadrilaterals

A **quadrilateral** is a 4-sided polygon. If you measure its angles and add them all up, you will always get 360°.

Here are a few examples of quadrilaterals.

1. Describe the lines and angles of each of the shapes to the person beside you. Can you name any of the quadrilaterals? Make or draw 4 quadrilaterals of your own.

> Can you see a repeated pattern?
> How would you describe it?

2. Discuss and name all of the shapes you can find on this house. How many shapes have you recorded altogether?

Trapezium

A **trapezium** is a 4-sided polygon that has exactly 1 pair of parallel sides. The 2 sides that are parallel are called the bases of the trapezium. The sum of the angles of a trapezium is 360°.

Here are a few examples. Try to make or draw some of your own.

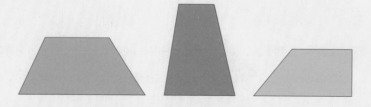

Tessellations

Look at the photograph.

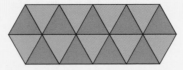
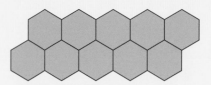

Tessellation of squares   Tessellation of triangles   Tessellation of hexagons

Tessellations or **tiling** means to arrange shapes in a repeated pattern so as to leave no spaces.

As you can see from the diagrams, squares, equilateral triangles and hexagons tessellate.

1. Make some tessellations using actual 2-D shapes.

2. Copy 1 of the above patterns onto squared paper and continue it across the page, leaving no spaces.

3. Not every 2-D shape tessellates. Can you predict which of these shapes will tessellate and which will not? Check your answers by drawing them.

	Tessellate: Yes/No
Circle	
Parallelogram	
Isosceles triangle	
Trapezium	
Pentagon	
Hexagon	
Rectangle	
Semi-circle	

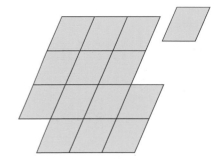

4. Draw this tessellation of a rhombus into your copy and continue the pattern. When finished, colour it in, making an interesting pattern.

5. Tessellations can be found in our environment. Think of 5 examples in your classroom, school or playground. Discuss with the person beside you. Does this shape tessellate?

6. Tessellations can be made using letters and numbers.

   a) Here is the letter T. Can you continue this tessellation?

   b) Find 2 letters and 2 numbers that tessellate and draw a small example of each.

7. Continue this tessellation.
   Design tessellating patterns from 2 other unusual shapes.

8. Take a really close look at this picture and describe what you see. Can you design a tessellated creation of your own?

Symmetry

Can you fold a rectangular piece of paper so that 1 half of the paper fits exactly into the other half? Have a go.

Is there more than 1 way you can fold it exactly in half?

If it can be done, we say that the shape is **symmetrical** and the different fold lines are called the lines of symmetry.

Try the same experiment using a square piece of paper. Did you get exactly the same result?

1. Are these pictures symmetrical? How many lines of symmetry can you find on each?

2. Make up your own definitions for a symmetrical shape and lines of symmetry.
   a) My definition of a symmetrical shape is a shape that …
   b) My definition of a line of symmetry is a line that …

3. Which of these shapes are symmetrical? Copy them and show their lines of symmetry.

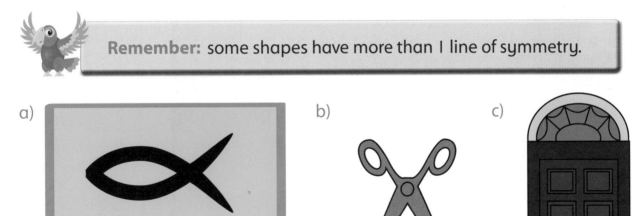

Remember: some shapes have more than 1 line of symmetry.

a)

b)

c)

d)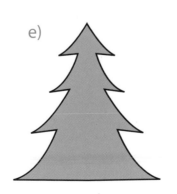

e)

f)

4. Find 10 objects in your classroom or school grounds that are symmetrical. Draw them on squared paper and show their lines of symmetry.

5. Letters and numbers can also be symmetrical. Which of these letters are symmetrical?

T D G R A C L Y

6. Draw the reflection of each of these shapes to make them symmetrical.

a)

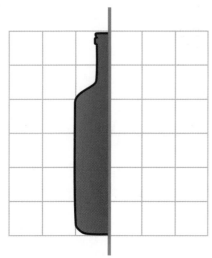

b)

c)

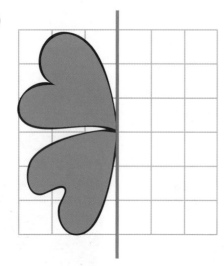

d)

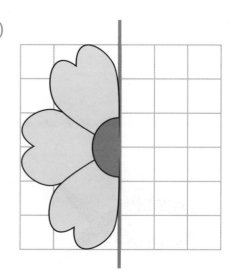

7. Draw and cut out each of the following shapes:

square, equilateral triangle, rectangle, trapezium, circle, hexagon

a) How many different ways can you fold each shape evenly in half?

b) Record your results by drawing the shape into your copy and drawing dotted lines where it has been folded.

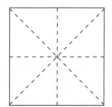

c) When you are finished folding and recording, you can use your findings to help you to complete this table.

Shape	Number of Sides	Number of Angles	Symmetrical? Yes or No	Number of Lines of Symmetry
Square				
Rectangle				
Equilateral triangle				
Trapezium				
Hexagon				

Tangrams

The **tangram** is a square that is cut up into 7 regular-shaped pieces. It originated a long time ago in China.

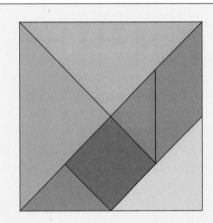

Each piece of the tangram is called a tan.

The 7 tans are:

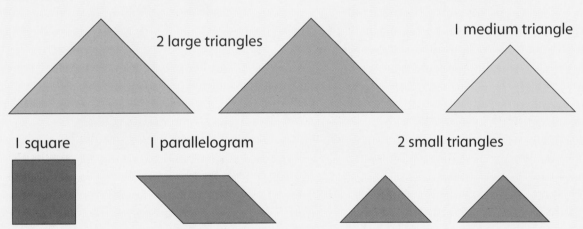

2 large triangles

1 medium triangle

1 square   1 parallelogram   2 small triangles

The classic rules when using tangrams to solve puzzles are:

1. All 7 tans must be used.
2. They must lay flat.
3. They must touch but may not overlap.

1. Use your tangrams to create the following shapes. Then design a few shapes of your own.

   a) Square

   b) Trapezium

   c) Right-angled isosceles triangle

2. Form the initials of your name using the tangram pieces.

Tantalizing Tangrams – Can You Make Them?

Homework

1. Sort this list of 2-D shapes into the table below.

> **Remember:** a polygon is a shape with the same number of sides as angles, while a regular polygon has equal sides and angles.

circle   parallelogram   rectangle   equilateral triangle   hexagon

rhombus   isosceles triangle   scalene triangle   pentagon   square

Polygon	Regular Polygon	Other

2. Draw equilateral, isosceles and scalene triangles in your copy. Write underneath them what makes them that type of triangle.

3. List as many different types of quadrilateral as you can. Draw examples of each one.

4. The following is a description of a rectangle:
   - It has 4 sides.
   - Opposite sides are equal.
   - Opposite sides are parallel.
   - All angles are right angles.

   How would you amend it to describe a trapezium?

Recap

- I can recognise and describe 2-D shapes. ○ ○ ○
- I know what regular polygons are. ○ ○ ○
- I can classify and describe triangles. ○ ○ ○
- I can identify different quadrilaterals. ○ ○ ○

11. Operations 2

 ## Talk About

Multiplication

Rounding up and rounding down can be very useful when we are estimating the answers to multiplication.

Bob bought 9 pencils that were 22c each. How much did the pencils cost altogether?

We can round 9 up to 10 and 22 down to 20.
So 10 × 20 = estimate.

1. Estimate the answers to these.

a) 11 apples @ 29c each   b) 81 grapes @ 9c each

c) 19 onions @ 42c each   d) 72 oranges @ 23c each

e) 63 peppers @ 57c each   f) 18 tomatoes @ 38c each

2. Estimate the answers before multiplying.

a) 139	b) 181	c) 248	d) 277	e) 304	f) 326
× 8	× 11	× 9	× 12	× 7	× 5

Strand: Number
Curriculum Objectives:
Estimate products and quotients of whole numbers;
divide a three-digit number by a two-digit number, without and with a calculator.

When we are multiplying by numbers greater than 12, there are 3 steps to the process.

First Step
We multiply by the units first.

4 × 7 units = 28 units

28 is made up of 2 tens and 8 units, so we put the 8 as our answer in the units column and put the 2 tens to the tens column.

4 × 5 tens = 20 tens and when we add in the extra 2 tens we get **22 tens**.

22 tens is made up of 2 hundreds and 2 tens, so we put 2 as our answer in the tens column and put the 2 hundreds to the hundreds column.

Finally, **4 × 2 hundreds = 8 hundreds**. When we add in the extra 2 hundreds, we get **10 hundreds**.

10 hundreds is made up of 1 thousand and 0 hundreds, so we put 0 as our answer in the hundreds column and 1 as our answer in the thousands column.

Th	H	T	U
	2	5	7
×		3_2	4
1	0	2	8

(× subscript 2 before 3)

Second Step
Now we multiply by the 3 tens. Because we are multiplying by tens, we will always have a 0 in the units column.

3 tens × 7 units = 21 tens, which is made up of 2 hundreds and 1 ten.

So we put the 1 ten in the tens column and carry the 2 hundreds to the hundreds column.

3 tens × 5 tens = 15 hundreds. When we add in the extra 2 hundreds we get a total of 17 hundreds, which is made up of 1 thousand and 7 hundreds. So we put the 7 hundreds in the hundreds column and put the 1 thousand to the thousands column.

Th	H	T	U
	2	5	7
×		3_2	4
1	0	2	8
7	^{17}	^{21}	0

Finally, 3 tens × 2 hundreds = 6 thousands. When we add in the extra 1 thousand we get a total of 7 thousands, which we record in the thousands column.

Third Step

To finish, we add the number we got when multiplying by the units to the number we got when multiplying by the tens.

0 units + 8 units = 8 units
I ten + 2 tens = 3 tens
7 hundreds + 0 hundreds = 7 hundreds
7 thousands + I thousand = 8 thousands

So 257 × 34 = 8738.

	Th	H	T	U
			2	5	7
×			₂3₂	4
	I	0	2	8
+	7	¹7	²I	0
	8	7	3	8

3. Now try these.

a) 152
   × 13

b) 188
   × 19

c) 313
   × 24

d) 269
   × 32

e) 422
   × 17

f) 348
   × 36

g) 219
   × 28

h) 174
   × 56

i) 271
   × 45

j) 189
   × 23

4. Use your calculator to find the answers to these questions.

a)   47
   × 23

b)   95
   × 17

c)   78
   × 34

d)   69
   × 28

e)   53
   × 16

f)   82
   × 45

g) 534
   × 76

h) 489
   × 92

i) 716
   × 37

j) 608
   × 59

k) 937
   × 65

l) 853
   × 48

Puzzler

Can you think of 2 numbers that are 4 times the sum of their digits?

5. A theatre holds 195 people. If a play runs for a fortnight and the theatre is full every night, how many people will have seen the play?

6. Find the product of 297 and 48.

7. Multiply the number of people in your class by the number of squares on a chessboard.

8. If a chocolate bar weighs 75g, what would 364 bars weigh?

9. Use your calculator to fill in this grid.

×	95	126	173	469	724
27					
18					

Division

A full box of pencils contains 8 pencils. If you have 288 pencils, how many boxes can you fill?

8 can be rounded up to 10 and 288 can be rounded up to 290.

So 8 $\overline{)288}$ 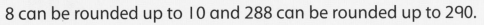 when rounded up becomes 10 $\overline{)290}$

Now make your estimate and check to see how close it was.

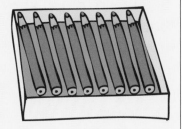

1. Estimate the answers to each of the following and then work out the answers.

   a) 9 $\overline{)189}$ b) 11 $\overline{)242}$ c) 8 $\overline{)552}$

   d) 7 $\overline{)399}$ e) 12 $\overline{)432}$ f) 6 $\overline{)714}$

   g) Which estimate was the least accurate? Why do you think that is? Discuss it with the people near you.

2. Now try these.
   a) 8 | 656
   b) 4 | 588
   c) 5 | 835
   d) 9 | 1251
   e) 12 | 1092
   f) 7 | 2492
   g) 7137 ÷ 9
   h) 6485 ÷ 5
   i) 5571 ÷ 3
   j) 9762 ÷ 6
   k) 4739 ÷ 7
   l) 2717 ÷ 11
   m) 8326 ÷ 10
   n) 9728 ÷ 9
   o) 5069 ÷ 12
   p) 3904 ÷ 7
   q) 6633 ÷ 8
   r) 7154 ÷ 4

3. Michael cycled 448km in 1 week. If he cycled exactly the same distance on each of the days, how far did he cycle each day?

4. If 9 people shared a prize of €6876, how much did each person get?

5. A shop sells golf balls in boxes containing 8 balls. How many boxes can be filled from 3798 balls? How many balls will be left over?

6. Mary earns €6996 a year. How much is she paid each month?

7. If a kangaroo can jump a distance of 11 metres and it needs to travel a distance of 8393 metres, how many jumps will it take?

Roy has a bag of 26 sweets. He wants to divide them equally between his 13 friends, but he is not sure how many sweets he should give to each of them. Can you help him?

If he gives 1 sweet to each of them, how many will he have left?

26 – 13 =

Does he have enough sweets left to give another sweet to each person? If he does, how many sweets will be left over?

We can work out the division of the sweets by subtracting as many times as we can. It could look like this:

$$
\begin{array}{r}
26 \\
-\ 13 \\
\hline
13 \\
-\ 13 \\
\hline
00
\end{array}
$$

The number of times we can subtract 13 is the number of sweets that each of the friends gets. **So 26 ÷ 13 = 2.**

If Roy had 42 sweets in the bag, how many sweets would each of his friends get? Would there be any sweets left over for Roy? Work it out by subtracting.

$$42 ÷ 13 = \underline{\quad} \ R \underline{\quad}$$

8. Divide these amounts of sweets out evenly. Work out the answers by subtracting as many times as you can. Write out the answers to the divisions at the end. Don't forget to include any sweets that might be left over.

   a) 48 sweets between 16 people
   b) 68 sweets between 17 people
   c) 59 sweets between 18 people
   d) 79 sweets between 15 people
   e) 161 sweets between 23 people
   f) 165 sweets between 19 people

What would be the problem if you were asked to divide 860 sweets between 20 people?

Try it.

```
      860
    − 20
    ─────
      840
    − 20
    ─────
      820
```

Do you give up yet? You'll be glad to know that there is a quicker way.

We know that 20 × 10 = 200, so every time we subtract 200 sweets, it's 10 sweets for each person.

```
      860
    − 200  (10)
    ─────
      660
    − 200  10)
    ─────
      460
    − 200  (10)
    ─────
      260
    − 200  10)
    ─────
       60
    −  20  (1)
    ─────
       40
    −  20  (1)
    ─────
       20
    −  20  (1)
```

So how many sweets does each person get?

$$860 ÷ 20 = 10 + 10 + 10 + 10 + 1 + 1 + 1 = 43$$

9. Work these out by subtracting. Find larger numbers to subtract to make it easier for yourself.

    a) 544 ÷ 17   b) 902 ÷ 22   c) 756 ÷ 18

Share a prize of €152 between 19 people.

Instead of subtracting over and over again, we could guess an amount to give each of them and see if it comes to €152.

$$19 \times €\underline{\hspace{1cm}} = €152$$

Round up and down to make a good estimate.

$$20 \times €\underline{\hspace{1cm}} = €150$$

What 2 numbers would be good guesses?
Try each to see which estimate is right.

$$\begin{array}{r} 19 \\ \times\ 7 \\ \hline 133 \end{array} \qquad \begin{array}{r} 19 \\ \times\ 8 \\ \hline 152 \end{array}$$

So each person would get €8, or €152 ÷ 19 = €8.

---

10. Try these by estimating first and then trying your estimates when multiplying.

    a) 18 × ___ = 126   b) 21 × ___ = 189   c) 29 × ___ = 145

    d) 23 × ___ = 138   e) 32 × ___ = 256   f) 28 × ___ = 252

Another way of writing 28 × ___ = 252 is 28 $\overline{)252}$. But because very few people know their 28 times tables, it's easier to work out the division by multiplying.

So 17 $\overline{)136}$ $^{008}$ is 17 × 8 = 136

Now we can estimate. Try the estimates in the multiplication and so find the answer to the division.

11. Now try these. (Hint: none of the answers are bigger than 9.)

a) $24\overline{)96}$

b) $22\overline{)132}$

c) $18\overline{)162}$

d) $27\overline{)135}$

e) $31\overline{)248}$

f) $16\overline{)112}$

g) $152 \div 38$

h) $287 \div 41$

i) $210 \div 35$

j) $392 \div 49$

k) $159 \div 53$

l) $290 \div 58$

As we know, sometimes numbers do not divide in exactly and we are left with a remainder.

$28\overline{)209}$ or $30 \times ? = 210$

So 7 is a good estimate.

| $\begin{array}{r} 28 \\ \times\ 7 \\ \hline 196 \end{array}$ | So let's try 8. | $\begin{array}{r} 28 \\ \times\ 8 \\ \hline 224 \end{array}$ | 8 is too big. |

So $\begin{array}{r} 28\overline{)209} \\ -\ 196 \\ \hline 13 \end{array}$ We work out the remainder by subtracting.

The answer is 7 R 13.

---

12. Now try these. Find the remainder by subtracting.

a) $298 \div 47$

b) $456 \div 61$

c) $318 \div 42$

d) $237 \div 39$

e) $356 \div 58$

f) $722 \div 91$

g) $638 \div 77$

h) $599 \div 63$

i) $205 \div 71$

j) $808 \div 93$

k) $446 \div 52$

l) $562 \div 78$

| $29 \times 10 =$ | $34 \times 20 =$ | $17 \times 50 =$ |
| $45 \times 30 =$ | $38 \times 20 =$ | $41 \times 60 =$ |

 Remember: when we multiply by a ten (10, 20, 30, etc.), the answer will always end with a 0.

Sometimes in a division question we will get answers with tens and units.

$$\begin{array}{r} 0\,1 \\ 17\,\overline{\smash{)}\,238} \end{array}$$

We see that 17 goes into 23 once, but that 1 is in the tens column. So it is really 17 × 10. Therefore, we subtract 170 to get our first remainder.

$$\begin{array}{r} 0\,1\,4 \\ 17\,\overline{\smash{)}\,238} \\ -\,170 \\ \hline 68 \\ -\,68 \\ \hline 00 \end{array}$$

Now we can estimate how many times 17 goes into 68 to get an answer in our units column. 17 × 4 = 68, so 4 is the answer in the units column.

13. Now try these. Remember: the first part of your answer will be in the tens column, so you will be estimating by multiplying by a 10.

a) 396 ÷ 22   b) 336 ÷ 24   c) 455 ÷ 35   d) 324 ÷ 18

e) 532 ÷ 28   f) 495 ÷ 15   g) 851 ÷ 37   h) 625 ÷ 25

i) 696 ÷ 29   j) 629 ÷ 17   k) 882 ÷ 21   l) 936 ÷ 26

m) 853 ÷ 27   n) 951 ÷ 16   o) 786 ÷ 33   p) 575 ÷ 38

q) 849 ÷ 45   r) 902 ÷ 53

14. How many times can you take 17 from 901?

15. Tony spent €576 buying 24 video games. How much did each game cost?

16. Amy saved €936 last year. If she saved the same amount each week, how much did she save every week?

17. Elaine's car needs 29 litres of petrol to fill her petrol tank. If she put 725 litres of petrol into her car last year, how many times did she fill the tank?

18. Fill in the blanks in this table.

Number of Items Bought	Cost of Item	Total Cost
27	€43	
39		€702
	€35	€805
56	€145	
226	€19	
	€33	€858
45		€720
28	€68	
13		€871
49	€294	

Try this one on your calculator: 625 ÷ 50.

What do you notice about your answer? What does this tell you?

Now let's work out the answer without the calculator.

```
      012
50 | 625
  −500
   125
  −100
    25
```

So the answer we get when we divide 625 by 50 is **12 R 25**.

But when you used your calculator, you should have got an answer of **12.5**.

12.5 is the same as **12 R 25** because the remainder of **25** is $\frac{1}{2}$ of the number we're dividing by: **50**. So **50** divides into **625 12$\frac{1}{2}$ times** and when we write that as a decimal, it's **12.5**.

19. Work these out on your calculator.

a) 196 ÷ 14   b) 437 ÷ 19   c) 841 ÷ 58

d) 816 ÷ 96   e) 684 ÷ 48   f) 763 ÷ 28

Homework

1. Estimate the answers before multiplying. Check your answers with a calculator.

   a) 152
      × 9

   b) 139
      × 11

   c) 118
      × 19

   d) 147
      × 21

   e) 203
      × 18

   f) 161
      × 32

   g) 248
      × 29

   h) 234
      × 25

   i) 282
      × 17

   j) 195
      × 34

   k) 389
      × 23

   l) 186
      × 38

2. Estimate the answers to these and then work out the answers.

   a) 8 ⌐152   b) 12 ⌐228   c) 9 ⌐441   d) 6 ⌐378   e) 11 ⌐539   f) 7 ⌐623

3. Now try these. Remember: there could be remainders.

   a) 1806 ÷ 7   b) 3192 ÷ 5   c) 3752 ÷ 8   d) 7526 ÷ 9
   e) 8195 ÷ 6   f) 4334 ÷ 11   g) 9540 ÷ 10   h) 8735 ÷ 7
   i) 5796 ÷ 12   j) 3438 ÷ 6   k) 7384 ÷ 8   l) 3456 ÷ 9

4. Try these by estimating first and then trying your estimates in the multiplication.

   a) 19 × ___ = 95   b) 22 × ___ = 154   c) 28 × ___ = 168
   d) 29 × ___ = 203   e) 31 × ___ = 248   f) 37 × ___ = 333

5. Now try these. (Hint: none of the answers are bigger than 9.)

   a) 128 ÷ 16   b) 168 ÷ 24   c) 130 ÷ 26   d) 144 ÷ 36   e) 378 ÷ 42   f) 168 ÷ 56

6. Now try these. Find the remainder by subtracting.

   a) 234 ÷ 25   b) 189 ÷ 23   c) 275 ÷ 34   d) 394 ÷ 47   e) 468 ÷ 65   f) 617 ÷ 86

7. Now try these. Remember: the first part of your answer will be in the tens column, so you will be estimating by multiplying by a 10 (there could be remainders).

   a) 255 ÷ 15   b) 648 ÷ 27   c) 392 ÷ 28   d) 408 ÷ 19   e) 625 ÷ 25   f) 527 ÷ 34

Recap

• I can estimate and calculate products.   ○ ○ ○

• I can estimate and calculate quotients.   ○ ○ ○

• I can do long division.   ○ ○ ○

12. Chance

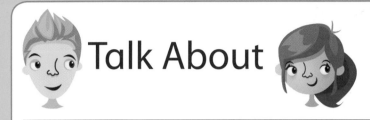

Psychic Sid can look into his crystal ball and predict what will happen in the future. He has never been wrong.
Here are his predictions for today.

- It will get dark tonight.
- It will rain again in the future.
- Someone in Ireland will have a cup of tea tomorrow.

1. What do you think of his predictions? Can you think of anything else that Sid could predict?

2. Some things aren't as easy to predict. Look at this list of predictions and state whether they are likely or unlikely to happen.

   a) It will rain tomorrow.

   b) The teacher will give you homework tonight.

   c) The teacher will give everyone in the class €20.

   d) The principal will come into the class today.

   e) Somebody in the class will sharpen their pencil today.

   f) Every time you toss a coin today, it will land showing heads.

3. Now write out the list of predictions in order, starting with the **most likely** event to happen and finishing with the **least likely**.

4. a) When you toss a coin, how many possible outcomes are there?

   b) If you tossed a coin 10 times, how often would you expect it to land on tails?

   c) Try it and see how accurate your prediction is. Keep a record to see how many times each one appears.

Heads	Tails
I I	I

Strand: Data
Curriculum Objectives:
Identify and list all possible outcomes of simple random processes;
estimate the likelihood of occurrence of events;
construct and use frequency charts and tables.

89

d) Now do exactly the same thing again. Was there any difference in the outcome?

e) What can we tell from this?

> Because there are 2 possible outcomes when you toss a coin, there is a 1 in 2 chance that the result will be heads and there is a 1 in 2 chance that the result will be tails.

5. a) This time, predict what the result of each toss will be. Then toss the coin to see if your prediction is right. Fill in this table to help you keep a record.

Toss	Prediction	Result	Right or Wrong
1			
2			
3			
4			
5			
6			
7			
8			
9			
10			

b) Try it with the person beside you. Did they toss exactly the same number of heads and tails as you did?

c) Which one of you got more predictions right?

6. a) If you tossed a coin 100 times, what would you expect the result to be?

b) Now get the results of 9 other people in the class and put them with your own to see what the result of 100 tosses would be. Record the number of heads and tails in your copy.

7. a) At the beginning of a football match, the referee tosses a coin between the 2 captains. The winning captain gets to choose in which direction his team is going to play. Is this a fair way to decide it?

b) Does the captain who gets to call heads or tails have an unfair advantage?

c) List some other fair ways of deciding who gets this advantage.

Greta, Gráinne and Grace were playing a guessing game. Greta asked Grace to guess the day of the week on which she was born. Gráinne asked Grace to guess the day of the week on which she started school. Grace thought that was fair because she had an equal chance of getting Greta and Gráinne's questions right, but Gráinne insisted that she had a greater chance of getting her question right. Who was right – Grace or Gráinne?

8. Put 3 markers or crayons (red, green and blue) in a bag. They should be the same size and shape. Without looking inside the bag, what are the chances of you picking out the red one?

   There is a ____ in ____ chance of picking out the red marker/crayon.

9. a) Pick 1 marker/crayon out 30 times. After each pick, put the marker/crayon back in the bag and give the bag a shake before making your next choice. Record which colour came out each time.

   b) How often should each colour be picked?

   c) Predict which colour will be picked out most often.

Colour	Number of Times Picked	Total
Red		
Blue		
Green		

10. This time, put 3 red markers, 2 blue markers and 1 green marker in a bag.

    What are the chances of you picking out a particular colour?

    a) There is a ____ in ____ chance of picking out the red marker.

    b) There is a ____ in ____ chance of picking out the blue marker.

    c) There is a ____ in ____ chance of picking out the green marker.

11. a) Pick a marker out of the bag 30 times, like you did before. Predict what colour you think it will be before you pick it out.

    b) Record your results and see how often you were right.

    c) How many times should you expect to be right?

Let's Play: What Are the Chances?

12. What are the chances of the following happening?

    a) Rolling a die and getting a 5.

    b) Picking the correct number in a raffle where the numbers are between 1 and 30.

    c) Picking the correct number in a raffle where the numbers are all the odd numbers between 10 and 40.

    d) Pointing to a black square on a chessboard while blindfolded.

    e) Picking a card from a deck of cards that is a club.

13. What are the chances of the following happening?

    a) Picking an ace from a deck of cards is a ___ in ___ chance.

    b) Picking a month in summer from a bag containing the names of the months of the year is a ___ in ___ chance.

    c) Today being a day that has an E in its name. (Be careful!)

14. A survey was conducted in a class to find out their favourite foods from a choice put to them. The choices were fruit, chocolate, cake and cheese. The results were as follows.

Food	Number of Children Who Prefer It
Fruit	7
Chocolate	11
Cake	9
Cheese	4

One of the children was asked to stand up.

a) What are the chances of that child having chosen cake as their preferred food?

b) What are the chances of that child having chosen cheese or chocolate as their preferred food?

c) The chances of picking a child who chose chocolate are exactly the same as picking a child who liked either _____ or _____.

15. Conduct a survey of your own and record the results in a table, as above. Write down the chances of the various options being taken.

Wheel of Fortune

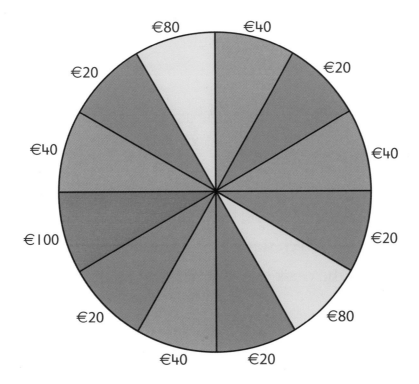

a) What prize are you most likely to win?

b) What are the chances of winning that prize?

c) What prize are you least likely to win?

d) What are the chances of winning that prize?

e) Why, do you think, is the wheel set up that way?

f) There is exactly the same chance of winning €____ as there is of winning either €____ or €____.

Homework

1. Put 2 playing cards into a bag.

    a) Ask somebody to pick 1 card out of the bag and record the result.

    b) Get the person to do it 10 times. Are the results what you expected?

    c) How often would you have expected each card to be picked?

2. Now put a 3rd card into the bag. Make sure each of the cards is a different suit.

    a) Now ask the person to pick out a card and again record the result.

    b) Do it 10 times. How did it affect the result?

    c) Was it what you expected?

3. a) Now change it by putting 2 cards of the same suit in the bag (say, diamonds) and 1 card of a different suit (say, clubs). How will this affect the result?

    b) What would you expect the result to be? Try it and see how it works out.

4. What are the chances of the following happening?

    a) Guessing the month in which someone's birthday falls is a ___ in ___ chance.

    b) Guessing the day of the week on which Christmas Day falls is a ___ in ___ chance.

    c) Picking a spade from a deck of playing cards (excluding the joker) is a ___ in ___ chance.

Recap

- I can determine the likelihood of particular outcomes. ◯ ◯ ◯

- I can establish the chance of a particular outcome happening. ◯ ◯ ◯

---

13. Fractions 2

Talk About

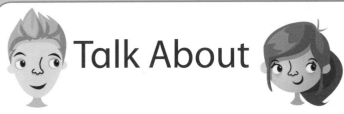

Estimating the Sum of 2 Fractions

Attention All Fraction Detectives

Take a piece of paper and fold it in half, then fold it in half again. Open it up and look at the different sections the page is divided into. What fraction is each one of these sections?

Now fold it back the way it was and fold it in half one more time. Open up the piece of paper again. What fraction of the page is each section now?

Has the amount of paper you have had in your hand changed at any stage during all this folding and opening? What conclusions might an ace fraction detective draw?

1. If John ate $\frac{1}{4}$ of a pizza and Jane ate $\frac{3}{4}$ of the pizza, how much pizza have they eaten between them?

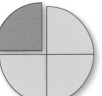

$$\frac{1}{4} + \frac{3}{4} = \text{---}$$

Trivia Question

When you add fractions with equal denominators, you only add the _____.

Is the answer:

a) numerators   b) denominators   c) alligators?

2. If Helen ate $\frac{3}{8}$ of a bar of chocolate and her friend Lisa ate $\frac{3}{8}$ of the bar, what fraction of the bar did they eat?

Shade in Lisa's fraction to find out how much they ate.

$$\frac{3}{8} + \frac{3}{8} = \text{---}$$

3. Try these. You can draw bars of chocolate to help.

a) $\frac{1}{5} + \frac{3}{5}$ b) $\frac{1}{7} + \frac{4}{7}$ c) $\frac{2}{9} + \frac{5}{9}$ d) $\frac{3}{8} + \frac{5}{8}$ e) $\frac{3}{11} + \frac{7}{11}$ f) $\frac{3}{10} + \frac{7}{10}$

g) Look at the answer to the last sum. Can you write the answer any other way?

Common Denominators

1. a) Longport County had a great season in the league and their strikers scored a lot of goals. Sniffer Smith scored $\frac{1}{2}$ of all their goals and Deadly Doyle scored $\frac{1}{4}$ of their goals. Between the 2 of them, what fraction of the team's goals did they score?

b) Estimate what fraction of the team's goals were scored by the 2 of them.

$$\frac{1}{2} + \frac{1}{4} = ?$$

Sniffer Smith

> If we knew how many quarters were in a half, we could add the fractions.
>
> $$\frac{1}{2} = \frac{2}{4} \qquad\qquad \frac{2}{4} \times \frac{1}{4} = \frac{3}{4}$$

2. See if you can add these fractions of the team's goals. From the size of the fractions, see if you can estimate what the answers will be.

a) $\frac{1}{2} + \frac{1}{6}$ b) $\frac{1}{4} + \frac{1}{8}$ c) $\frac{1}{3} + \frac{1}{6}$ d) $\frac{1}{8} + \frac{1}{2}$

To add fractions, we need them to have the same denominator. We call this a **common denominator**.

If Joe spent $\frac{1}{3}$ of his money on a T-shirt and $\frac{1}{4}$ of his money on a cap, what fraction of his money did he spend altogether? Draw the fractions to help you estimate the answer.

We have to find equivalent fractions of $\frac{1}{3}$ and $\frac{1}{4}$ that have the same denominator.

So what is the lowest common multiple of 3 and 4? Write out the list of multiples to help you.

3: 3, 6, 9, ⑫
4: 4, 8, ⑫   LCM = 12

Now make equivalent fractions of $\frac{1}{3}$ and $\frac{1}{4}$ with the lowest common multiple as their denominator. Remember to multiply by a member of the family of 1.

$$\frac{1}{3} \times \frac{4}{4} = \frac{4}{12} \qquad\qquad \frac{1}{4} \times \frac{3}{3} = \frac{3}{12}$$

Now you can add the fractions because you have the same denominator.

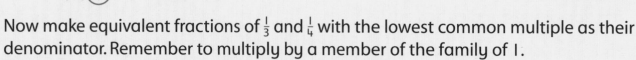

Adding Fractions

1. Now try these. Remember to change the fractions so that they have the same denominator. Estimate the answers first.

a) $\frac{1}{2} + \frac{1}{3}$ b) $\frac{1}{4} + \frac{1}{6}$ c) $\frac{1}{2} + \frac{1}{5}$ d) $\frac{1}{3} + \frac{1}{5}$

e) $\frac{1}{4} + \frac{1}{5}$ f) $\frac{1}{3} + \frac{1}{8}$ g) $\frac{1}{6} + \frac{1}{9}$ h) $\frac{1}{6} + \frac{1}{8}$

i) $\frac{1}{5} + \frac{1}{12}$ j) $\frac{1}{3} + \frac{1}{10}$ k) $\frac{1}{10} + \frac{1}{4}$ l) $\frac{1}{6} + \frac{1}{12}$

What did you notice about the LCM when you added $\frac{1}{6} + \frac{1}{12}$?

What can we say about this? Discuss.

Now look at the answer $\frac{3}{12}$.

Is there anything you can do to it?

Add these fractions in the same way as you did before.

$$\frac{3}{4} + \frac{2}{3}$$

What do you notice about your answer? Can you write your answer in a different way?

---

2. Try these. Write your answers both ways.

a) $\frac{2}{5} + \frac{7}{10}$ b) $\frac{3}{4} + \frac{3}{8}$ c) $\frac{5}{6} + \frac{3}{8}$ d) $\frac{4}{7} + \frac{4}{5}$ e) $\frac{5}{6} + \frac{5}{9}$

f) $\frac{3}{4} + \frac{4}{5}$ g) $\frac{5}{7} + \frac{2}{3}$ h) $\frac{9}{10} + \frac{5}{8}$ i) $\frac{5}{12} + \frac{5}{6}$

3. Jane drank $\frac{2}{3}$ of a bottle of orange. Samantha drank $\frac{1}{4}$ of it. How much of the bottle did they drink?

4. If a boy spent $\frac{2}{5}$ of his money on rhubarb and $\frac{3}{11}$ of his money on paper clips, what fraction of his money did he spend?

5. If Liam ate $\frac{4}{7}$ of a pizza and Jenny ate $\frac{2}{9}$ of it, what fraction of the pizza is left?

6. Tom's camán is $\frac{3}{4}$ of a metre long. Tim's camán is $\frac{1}{9}$ of a metre longer. How long is Tim's camán?

Subtracting Fractions

If Anne cuts a pizza into 8 equal slices but she feels full after eating 7 of the slices, what fraction of the pizza is left?

Each slice $= \frac{1}{8}$

So $1 - \frac{7}{8} = $____

Or $\frac{8}{8} - \frac{7}{8} = $____

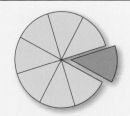

Just like when we add fractions, when we subtract fractions with equal denominators, you subtract only the _____.

---

1. Now try these. Remember to change the whole into a member of the family of 1.
   a) $1 - \frac{1}{4}$
   b) $1 - \frac{4}{7}$
   c) $1 - \frac{7}{10}$
   d) $1 - \frac{2}{3}$
   e) $1 - \frac{5}{9}$
   f) $1 - \frac{3}{8}$
   g) $1 - \frac{5}{12}$
   h) $1 - \frac{3}{11}$
   i) $1 - \frac{1}{6}$

2. If Jill spent $\frac{2}{9}$ of her money, what fraction had she left?

3. From a metre stick, a piece measuring $\frac{4}{11}$ of a metre was broken off. What fraction of the metre stick did the very cross teacher have left?

If you cut $\frac{1}{5}$ of a metre from a piece of string that is $\frac{3}{4}$ of a metre long, what length of string is left?

$$\frac{3}{4} - \frac{1}{5} =$$

We can subtract only fractions that have the same denominator, so what is the LCM of 4 and 5?

4: 4, 8, 12, 16, ⨀20
5: 5, 10, 15, ⨀20

Now make equivalent fractions of $\frac{3}{4}$ and $\frac{1}{5}$ with the LCM as their denominator. Remember to multiply by a member of the family of 1.

$$\frac{3}{4} \times \frac{5}{5} = \frac{15}{20} \qquad\qquad \frac{1}{5} \times \frac{4}{4} = \frac{4}{20}$$

Now you can subtract. How much string was left?

---

4. See if you can work these out. Remember to find the LCM of the denominators so that you can make equivalent fractions with the same denominator.
   a) $\frac{7}{8} - \frac{1}{4}$
   b) $\frac{7}{9} - \frac{1}{3}$
   c) $\frac{3}{4} - \frac{1}{2}$
   d) $\frac{4}{6} - \frac{2}{3}$
   e) $\frac{9}{10} - \frac{4}{5}$
   f) $\frac{8}{11} - \frac{3}{8}$
   g) $\frac{5}{6} - \frac{3}{4}$
   h) $\frac{7}{12} - \frac{4}{7}$
   i) $\frac{8}{9} - \frac{5}{6}$

5. If Peter ate $\frac{7}{8}$ of his pizza and Niamh ate $\frac{3}{5}$ of her pizza, how much more pizza did Peter eat?

6. From a piece of wood $\frac{5}{8}$ of a metre long, I cut off a piece measuring $\frac{2}{5}$ of a metre. What fraction of a metre do I have left?

Homework

1. Try these. Remember: only add the numerators.

   a) $\frac{1}{4} + \frac{3}{4}$ b) $\frac{1}{5} + \frac{4}{5}$ c) $\frac{5}{8} + \frac{1}{8}$ d) $\frac{5}{9} + \frac{2}{9}$ e) $\frac{2}{7} + \frac{3}{7}$ f) $\frac{1}{6} + \frac{5}{6}$

2. From the size of the fractions, see if you can estimate what the answers will be.

   a) $\frac{1}{4} + \frac{1}{3}$ b) $\frac{3}{4} + \frac{1}{8}$ c) $\frac{1}{2} + \frac{1}{10}$ d) $\frac{3}{8} + \frac{1}{4}$

3. Now try these. Remember to change the fractions so that they have the same denominator. Estimate the answers first.

   a) $\frac{1}{3} + \frac{1}{6}$ b) $\frac{1}{4} + \frac{1}{8}$ c) $\frac{1}{3} + \frac{1}{9}$ d) $\frac{1}{4} + \frac{1}{12}$ e) $\frac{1}{5} + \frac{1}{6}$ f) $\frac{1}{5} + \frac{1}{8}$

4. Try these. Write your answers both ways.

   a) $\frac{2}{3} + \frac{7}{9}$ b) $\frac{3}{4} + \frac{5}{6}$ c) $\frac{3}{4} + \frac{7}{8}$ d) $\frac{7}{9} + \frac{5}{6}$ e) $\frac{7}{8} + \frac{1}{6}$ f) $\frac{7}{12} + \frac{5}{8}$

5. Now try these. Remember to change the whole into the relevant member of the family of 1.

   a) $1 - \frac{5}{6}$ b) $1 - \frac{7}{9}$ c) $1 - \frac{5}{8}$ d) $1 - \frac{3}{4}$ e) $1 - \frac{3}{5}$ f) $1 - \frac{9}{10}$

6. See if you can work these out. Remember to find the LCM of the denominators so that you can make equivalent fractions with the same denominator.

   a) $\frac{7}{10} - \frac{2}{5}$ b) $\frac{5}{6} - \frac{1}{4}$ c) $\frac{3}{4} - \frac{5}{8}$ d) $\frac{8}{9} - \frac{2}{3}$ e) $\frac{7}{8} - \frac{5}{6}$ f) $\frac{9}{10} - \frac{3}{4}$

Recap

- I can estimate the sum of 2 fractions.   ○ ○ ○

- I can find common denominators for fractions.   ○ ○ ○

- I can add fractions.   ○ ○ ○

- I can subtract fractions.   ○ ○ ○

14. Number Theory 2

Talk About

Tired of Checking for Primes?

Is 97 a prime number? It's hard to say without dividing a lot of different numbers into 97 to see if they are factors.

How would you like to know if a number was prime or not without having to think about it?

Just follow these instructions carefully and you will be able to tell all the prime numbers from 1 to 100 at a glance.

First draw a 100-square like this one into your copy.

Now cross out 1 because it is not a prime number.

Put a circle around 2 because it is a prime number.

Now cross out all the multiples of 2 (count up in 2s) because they are _____ numbers.

1	2	3	4	5	6	7	8	9	10
11	12	13	14	15	16	17	18	19	20
21	22	23	24	25	26	27	28	29	30
31	32	33	34	35	36	37	38	39	40
41	42	43	44	45	46	47	48	49	50
51	52	53	54	55	56	57	58	59	60
61	62	63	64	65	66	67	68	69	70
71	72	73	74	75	76	77	78	79	80
81	82	83	84	85	86	87	88	89	90
91	92	93	94	95	96	97	98	99	100

Put a circle around 3 and then cross out all the multiples of 3. (Some of them will already be crossed out.)

Put a circle around 5 and then cross out all the multiples of 5. (Again, some of them will already be crossed out.)

Put a circle around 7 and then cross out the multiples of 7.

Now circle all the remaining numbers that have not been crossed off.

All the prime numbers between 1 and 100 now have a circle around them.

This is called the **sieve of Eratosthenes**, after the Greek mathematician who devised this method of 'sieving' out the prime numbers.

1. Use the sieve to find out if this statement is **true** or **false**: All prime numbers are odd numbers.

Strand: Number
Curriculum Objectives:
Identify simple prime and composite numbers;
identify square and rectangular numbers.

Rectangular Numbers

Most numbers can be arranged to make particular shapes.
The factors of 8 are 2 × 4, so on a pegboard we arrange 8 pegs into 2 rows of 4.

1. a) What shape does this give us?
   b) Could it be arranged in any other way? If so, how?

2. Using a pegboard, geoboard or simply the squares in your copy, arrange these numbers into rectangular shapes by using their factors.

   10   15   21   14   27   35

Numbers that have many factors can be arranged into more than 1 rectangular shape.

$2 \times 6 = 12$  $3 \times 4 = 12$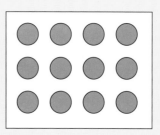

3. See how many different ways you can arrange the following numbers into rectangular shapes.

   18   20   24   30   36   40

Puzzler

A set of football matches is to be organised in a round robin fashion: every participating team plays a match against every other team once and only once.

If 55 matches in total are played, how many teams participated?

Square Numbers

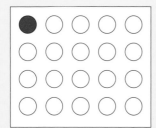   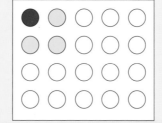   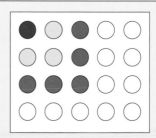

Continue the sequence on your own pegboard. What do you notice about the shape of each of the numbers? We call each of these numbers square numbers.

They can also be worked out by multiplying each of the numbers by themselves.

$1 \times 1 = 1$, $2 \times 2 = 4$, $3 \times 3 = 9$ and so on.

So the first square number is 1, the second is 4 and so on.

4. Work out what these square numbers would be.
   a) What is the 6th square number?
   b) What is the 9th square number?
   c) What is the 14th square number?
   d) What is the 17th square number?
   e) What is the 25th square number?
   f) What is the 28th square number?

Square numbers can be written as follows:
$7^2 = 7 \times 7 = 49$

5. Work out the following squares.
   a) 5^2
   b) 9^2
   c) 8^2
   d) 4^2
   e) 10^2
   f) 6^2

Homework

1. Use your sieve of Eratosthenes to identify if the following numbers are prime.
   a) 21
   b) 31
   c) 47
   d) 57
   e) 61
   f) 79

2. See how many different ways you can arrange the following numbers into rectangular shapes.
   a) 16
   b) 22
   c) 27
   d) 30
   e) 32
   f) 48

3. a) What is the 5th square number?
   b) What is the 8th square number?
   c) What is the 12th square number?
   d) What is the 19th square number?
   e) What is the 24th square number?
   f) What is the 30th square number?

Recap

- I can use the sieve of Eratosthenes to identify prime numbers.

- I can identify rectangular numbers.

- I can identify square numbers.

- I can calculate square numbers.

15. The Circle

 ## Talk About

Have a look around the classroom and find as many examples of circles as you can.

Can you fill in the blanks for this definition of a circle?

A circle is a line that is made up of many points that are the _____ distance from the _____ point.

1. Draw 3 circles in your copy, each with a different diameter.

   a) Draw a circle by tracing around a circular object.

   b) Draw a circle using a pencil, pin and string.

   c) Draw a circle using your compass.

   d) Measure the diameter of each circle with your ruler.

Strand: Shape and Space
Curriculum Objectives:
Identify the properties of the circle;
construct a circle of given radius or diameter.

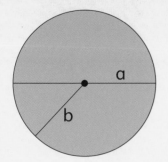

Look at these circles and discuss the different parts and names for each.

The point in the middle of the circle is called the _____.

The line (a) going from 1 side of the circle to another, passing through the centre of the circle, is called the **diameter**.

The line (b) joining the centre point to the circumference is called the **radius**.

2. Draw a circle into your copy and label the different parts.

Draw a large circle on a piece of paper and cut it out. Find the centre point by folding it in half twice, opening it out and marking where the 4 lines meet.

Measure the fold line from the centre point to the edge of the circle, the radius.

Measure the fold line from 1 edge of the circle to the other, the diameter.

Can you work out a relationship between the diameter and the radius?

diameter   radius

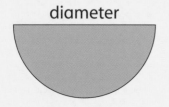 

diameter = _____ radii

3. What is the diameter of each of these circles?

a) radius 3cm   b) radius 11cm   c) radius 2.5cm

d) radius 6.1cm   e) radius 7cm   f) radius 4.9cm

g) radius 12.2cm   h) radius 8.5cm   i) radius $5\frac{1}{2}$cm

4. Find the radius of each of these circles if the diameter is:

a) 16cm   b) 24cm   c) 12.8cm

d) 10.2cm   e) 30.6cm   f) 11cm

g) 25cm   h) 19.2cm   i) $8\frac{1}{2}$cm

5. Using your compass, construct circles with the following radii.

a) 4cm   b) 3.5cm   c) 2cm   d) 5.2cm   e) 3cm

6. Using your compass, construct circles with the following diameters.

a) 10cm   b) 6.2cm   c) 5cm   d) 9cm   e) 8.6cm

7. Find the approximate area of this circle by counting the number of squares it encloses.

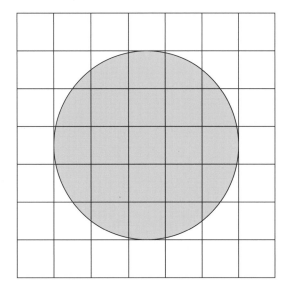

Count the full squares enclosed: _____

Count the squares in which half or more is enclosed and add them: _____
(For example, 2 half squares = 1 full square.)

Add your answers together to get the approximate area: _____ cm²

8. Find the approximate area of these circles in the same way.

a)

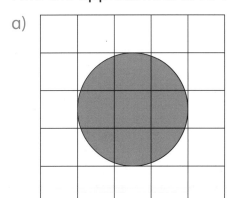

b)

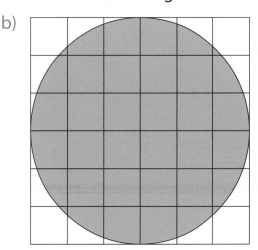

9. Draw the following circles on centimetre square paper and estimate the area of each.
   a) 4cm radius   b) 2cm radius   c) 3cm radius   d) 5cm radius

Circle Designs

Many designs can be made using circles. Study how the following examples were made and try a few of your own.

 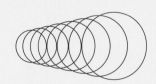  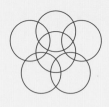

Homework

1. Place these labels in the right places on the circle.

   radius   diameter

2. Fill in the blanks in this table.

	Radius	Diameter
Circle A	26cm	
Circle B		39cm
Circle C		142.8cm
Circle D	6.75m	
Circle E	1.298km	
Circle F		33.7cm

3. Using your compass, construct circles with the following radii.
   a) 4.5cm   b) 5cm   c) 3.8cm

4. Using your compass, construct circles with the following diameters.
   a) 8cm   b) 12cm   c) 7cm

Recap

- I know the different parts of the circle.   ◯ ◯ ◯

- I know that the radius of a circle is half of the diameter.   ◯ ◯ ◯

- I know how to estimate the area of a circle.   ◯ ◯ ◯

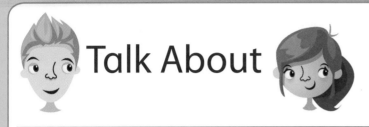

Talk About

Fraction Wall (1, $\frac{1}{2}$, $\frac{1}{4}$, $\frac{1}{8}$, $\frac{1}{12}$)

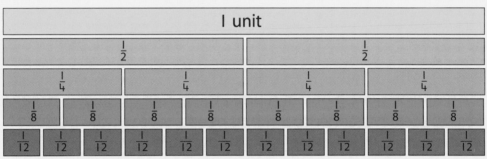

Fill in the blanks to make equivalent fractions. Use the fraction wall to help you.

$$1 \text{ whole} = \frac{}{4} \qquad \frac{1}{2} = \frac{}{4} \qquad \frac{1}{4} = \frac{}{8}$$

$$\frac{}{2} = \frac{4}{8} \qquad \frac{}{4} = \frac{6}{8} \qquad \frac{}{4} = 1 \text{ whole}$$

Fraction Wall (1, $\frac{1}{3}$, $\frac{1}{6}$, $\frac{1}{9}$, $\frac{1}{12}$)

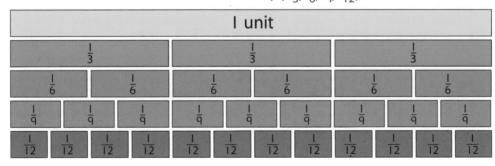

1. Look at each pair of fractions and decide which fraction is bigger or if they are equivalent. Use the fraction wall to help you.

   a) $\frac{1}{3}$ and $\frac{5}{9}$

   b) $\frac{1}{6}$ and $\frac{2}{3}$

   c) $\frac{5}{6}$ and $\frac{7}{9}$

   d) $\frac{6}{9}$ and $\frac{2}{3}$

   e) $\frac{2}{6}$ and $\frac{4}{9}$

   f) $\frac{4}{6}$ and $\frac{6}{9}$

   g) $\frac{2}{3}$ and $\frac{3}{6}$

   h) $\frac{4}{9}$ and $\frac{3}{6}$

   i) $\frac{8}{9}$ and $\frac{5}{6}$

Strand: Number
Curriculum Objectives:
Compare and order fractions and identify equivalent forms of fractions with denominators 2–12;
express improper fractions as mixed numbers and vice versa and position them on the number line;
add and subtract simple mixed numbers.

Puzzler

At a birthday party, one-half drank only orange juice, one-third drank only apple juice, 9 people drank neither and nobody drank both. How many people were at the party?

2. Put these mixed numbers onto the number line.

$1\frac{1}{2}$, $1\frac{5}{8}$, $1\frac{3}{4}$, $1\frac{1}{8}$, $1\frac{1}{4}$, $1\frac{7}{8}$, $1\frac{3}{8}$

John had a party and he gave a half of a pizza to each of his guests to eat. If he needed $3\frac{1}{2}$ pizzas to feed everyone, how many people were at the party?

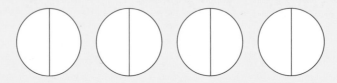

Divide the pizzas in half and count the halves.

$$3\frac{1}{2} = \frac{7}{2}$$

Raymond had a party the following week, but he wasn't as generous and gave his guests only $\frac{1}{4}$ of a pizza each. If he needed $2\frac{3}{4}$ pizzas to feed everyone, how many people were at his party?

Draw the pizzas to help you. Remember: $\frac{4}{4}$ makes 1 full pizza.

$$2\frac{3}{4} = \frac{}{4}$$

Change Mixed Numbers into Improper Fractions

Can you detect a quicker way of doing problems like these? Talk about it in pairs.

1. Now try these the quicker way.

a) $1\frac{1}{5} = \frac{}{5}$

b) $1\frac{2}{3} = \frac{}{3}$

c) $2\frac{1}{2} = \frac{}{2}$

d) $1\frac{3}{4} = \frac{}{4}$

e) $2\frac{1}{3} = \frac{}{3}$

f) $3\frac{1}{6} = \frac{}{6}$

g) $2\frac{3}{5} = \frac{}{5}$

h) $1\frac{5}{9} = \frac{}{9}$

i) $2\frac{5}{8} = \frac{}{8}$

j) $5\frac{1}{4} = \frac{}{4}$

k) $7\frac{1}{2} = \frac{}{2}$

l) $4\frac{2}{7} = \frac{}{7}$

Change Improper Fractions into Mixed Numbers

At the end of his party, John decided that his 7 guests were quite full after the pizza, so he gave them each $\frac{1}{5}$ of a cake. How many full cakes and extra slices did he need?

7 slices of $\frac{1}{5}$ of a cake gives you 1 full cake and 2 slices.

$$\frac{7}{5} = 1\frac{2}{5}$$

Raymond's 11 guests were still a bit peckish, so he decided to give them $\frac{1}{3}$ of a cake each. How many full cakes and extra slices did he need? Draw the cakes to help you work it out.

11 slices of $\frac{1}{3}$ of a cake gives you ____ full cakes and ____ slices.

$$\frac{11}{3} = \frac{\quad}{3}$$

Have the detectives among you worked out a quicker way to solve problems like these?

1. Now try these the quicker way.

a) $\frac{9}{8} =$ b) $\frac{10}{7} =$ c) $\frac{5}{2} =$ d) $\frac{9}{4} =$

e) $\frac{8}{3} =$ f) $\frac{12}{5} =$ g) $\frac{11}{6} =$ h) $\frac{16}{3} =$

i) $\frac{21}{11} =$ j) $\frac{25}{12} =$ k) $\frac{27}{8} =$ l) $\frac{35}{4} =$

m) $\frac{48}{7} =$ n) $\frac{56}{9} =$ o) $\frac{17}{9} =$ p) $\frac{83}{10} =$

q) $\frac{65}{9} =$ r) $\frac{73}{8} =$ s) $\frac{53}{12} =$ t) $\frac{72}{6} =$

Puzzler

If every player on a rugby team got $\frac{1}{4}$ of an orange at halftime, how many oranges would the team need exactly?

What's the crucial bit of information that we need to know?

Write Whole Numbers as Improper Fractions

If there are 3 thirds in 1 whole block of ice cream, how many thirds are there in 3 blocks?

 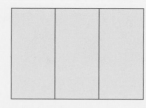 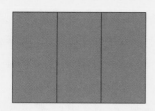

$$3 = \frac{9}{3}$$

If I cut 6 apples into quarters, how many quarters will I have altogether?

Draw the apples if it helps you.

$$6 = \frac{}{4}$$

Can you see a quick way of working it out? Why does this work?

1. Now fill in the missing numerators.

a) $5 = \frac{}{2}$ b) $4 = \frac{}{7}$ c) $10 = \frac{}{5}$ d) $7 = \frac{}{6}$

e) $\frac{}{8} = 9$ f) $\frac{}{3} = 12$ g) $\frac{}{11} = 7$ h) $\frac{}{4} = 9$

i) $7 = \frac{}{10}$ j) $6 = \frac{}{9}$ k) $\frac{}{12} = 5$ l) $\frac{}{8} = 8$

2. **Mixed Numbers**

   Improper Fractions

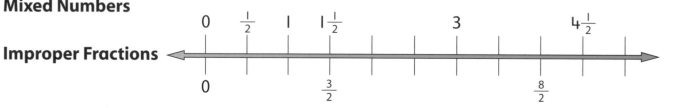

a) Can you fill in the gaps above and below this number line?

b) Extend the number line as far as 8.

c) How many spaces are there between each whole number (between 0 and 1)?

d) If you divided the space between each whole number into quarters, how many spaces would there be between each whole number?

3. Draw a number line from 0 to 3 and divide it up into quarters. Now write in the mixed numbers above the number line and the improper fractions below it. Answer the following questions based on the number line.

a) How many quarters are there in $2\frac{1}{4}$?

b) If you add $\frac{3}{4}$ to $1\frac{3}{4}$, where will you be on the number line?

c) If you extend the number line, how many wholes and how many spare quarters are the same as $\frac{15}{4}$?

Adding Mixed Numbers

If John eats $1\frac{1}{2}$ bars of chocolate and Tom eats $1\frac{1}{4}$ bars, how many bars have they eaten altogether?

There is more than 1 way of working this out. Look at the bars of chocolate and see if you can spot the different ways. Discuss it with the person nearest to you.

Now try each of the ways you have found and see if you come up with the same answer.

Option 1

$1\frac{1}{2} + 1\frac{1}{4}$

$\frac{3}{2} + \frac{5}{4}$

$\frac{6}{4} + \frac{5}{4}$

$\frac{11}{4} = 2\frac{3}{4}$

Option 2

$1\frac{1}{2} + 1\frac{1}{4}$

$2(\frac{1}{2} + \frac{1}{4})$

$2(\frac{2}{4} + \frac{1}{4})$

$2\frac{3}{4}$

1. Work out the answers to these. You can do them whichever way you prefer.

    a) $1\frac{1}{6} + \frac{2}{3}$

    b) $1\frac{1}{3} + 4\frac{5}{9}$

    c) $2\frac{1}{4} + 1\frac{3}{8}$

    d) $3\frac{1}{2} + 1\frac{2}{5}$

    e) $2\frac{1}{6} + 3\frac{5}{12}$

    f) $1\frac{1}{9} + 1\frac{5}{6}$

    g) $7\frac{2}{5} + 3\frac{1}{3}$

    h) $6\frac{7}{8} + 1\frac{2}{3}$

    i) $4\frac{5}{6} + 1\frac{1}{3}$

    j) What did you notice about your answers to the last 2 sums? Discuss what you did with the people near you.

2. If a woman worked for $4\frac{1}{4}$ hours in the morning and $3\frac{3}{5}$ hours in the afternoon, how long did she spend working?

3. In a long jump competition, a boy jumped a distance of $3\frac{5}{6}$ metres in the first round. If his second jump was $\frac{3}{8}$ of a metre further than his first jump, what distance did he jump in the second round?

Subtracting Mixed Numbers

If Jim is $1\frac{3}{4}$ metres tall and Frank is $1\frac{1}{2}$ metres tall, what is the difference in their height?

$$1\frac{3}{4} - 1\frac{1}{2} =$$

Yes, you've guessed it: there is more than one way of doing this one as well! (Hint: it's just like addition.)

Try each of the ways and see which one you prefer. See if you get the same answer each time.

1. Now try these.

   a) $1\frac{7}{8} - 1\frac{3}{4}$

   b) $1\frac{5}{9} - 1\frac{1}{3}$

   c) $2\frac{7}{10} - 1\frac{2}{5}$

   d) $3\frac{3}{4} - 1\frac{1}{6}$

   e) $4\frac{6}{7} - 2\frac{3}{5}$

   f) $8\frac{2}{3} - 5\frac{7}{12}$

If a bucket contains $1\frac{1}{6}$ litres of water and I pour $\frac{2}{3}$ of a litre out of the bucket, how much water is left in the bucket?

$$1\frac{1}{6} - \frac{2}{3} = 1\frac{1}{6} - \frac{4}{6}$$

Can you spot a problem? How could you solve this problem? Talk about it with the person nearest you. (Hint: you need to borrow – but from where?)

Work out the answer. Remember to reduce your answer to its lowest terms.

2. Now try these.

   a) $1\frac{1}{4} - \frac{1}{2}$

   b) $1\frac{3}{8} - \frac{3}{4}$

   c) $2\frac{3}{5} - 1\frac{9}{10}$

   d) $4\frac{1}{9} - 1\frac{1}{6}$

   e) $5\frac{1}{12} - 2\frac{3}{8}$

   f) $3\frac{2}{5} - 1\frac{3}{4}$

3. Amy spent $3\frac{1}{4}$ hours in her bedroom. If she spent $\frac{5}{6}$ of an hour watching TV and the rest of the time reading, how long did she spend reading? When you get your answer as a fraction, change it to hours and minutes.

Find a Fraction of an Amount

Tom got €36 for his birthday and he spent $\frac{1}{4}$ of it on a new T-shirt. How much did the T-shirt cost?

What do we know?

€36

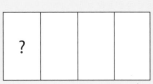

We know that all of his money is €36. $\frac{4}{4} = €36$

We want to find $\frac{1}{4}$ of his money. $\frac{1}{4} = €?$

To find $\frac{1}{4}$ of something, we divide by 4. $36 \div 4$

So the T-shirt cost €9.

1. Find:

   a) $\frac{1}{2}$ of €44
   b) $\frac{1}{5}$ of €35
   c) $\frac{1}{3}$ of €87
   d) $\frac{1}{8}$ of €120

   e) $\frac{1}{7}$ of €147
   f) $\frac{1}{10}$ of €230
   g) $\frac{1}{6}$ of €192
   h) $\frac{1}{9}$ of €162

2. Use your calculator to work these out.

   a) $\frac{1}{9}$ of 324
   b) $\frac{1}{6}$ of 234
   c) $\frac{1}{8}$ of 376
   d) $\frac{1}{11}$ of 638

   e) $\frac{1}{7}$ of 966
   f) $\frac{1}{4}$ of 1132
   g) $\frac{1}{12}$ of 1020
   h) $\frac{1}{5}$ of 1695

Jane got €42 for her birthday and spent $\frac{2}{3}$ of it on CDs. How much money did she spend?

€42

We know $\frac{3}{3} = €42$.

We know that to find $\frac{1}{3}$, we divide by 3. $42 \div 3 = 14$

We know $\frac{2}{3}$ is twice as much as $\frac{1}{3}$, so: $14 \times 2 = 28$

Look at the number we divided by and the number we multiplied by. Now look back at the fraction in the question. What do you notice?

Devise a rule for finding a fraction of a number with the people near you.

3. Find:

   a) $\frac{3}{4}$ of €28
   b) $\frac{4}{9}$ of €117
   c) $\frac{3}{5}$ of €135
   d) $\frac{7}{10}$ of €180

   e) $\frac{5}{6}$ of €138
   f) $\frac{7}{8}$ of €232
   g) $\frac{6}{11}$ of €121
   h) $\frac{5}{12}$ of €288

4. In a long jump competition, Mary's first jump was 348cm long. If Lisa's first jump was $\frac{3}{4}$ of the length of Mary's, how far did Lisa jump?

5. While on holidays, Mark collected 245 seashells. He gave $\frac{2}{5}$ of them to his brother. How many shells had he left?

6. There are 632 children in a school. If $\frac{3}{8}$ of them are boys, how many girls are there?

7. If a lady had €456 and she spent $\frac{7}{12}$ of it on a TV, work out how much the TV cost and how much money she had left. Discuss with the people near you how many different ways there are of doing this problem.

Find the Whole Amount from a Fraction

1. a) $\frac{1}{2}$ of my money is €25. All of my money is €_____.

    b) $\frac{1}{4}$ of my money is €36. All of my money is €_____.

    c) $\frac{1}{3}$ of my money is €18. All of my money is €_____.

    d) $\frac{1}{5}$ of my money is €20. All of my money is €_____.

    e) $\frac{1}{6}$ of my money is €15. All of my money is €_____.

    f) $\frac{1}{8}$ of my money is €18. All of my money is €_____.

Ian spent $\frac{4}{5}$ of his money buying a skateboard. If the skateboard cost €36, how much money had he altogether?

= €36   = €?

What do we know?

We know that $\frac{4}{5}$ of his money is €36. $\frac{4}{5}$ = €36

We want to work out how much money he had altogether. $\frac{5}{5}$ = €?

First we must work out $\frac{1}{5}$. $\frac{1}{5}$ = 36 ÷ 4 = 9

                                                               $\frac{5}{5}$ = 9 × 5 = 45

---

2. Now work out the whole amount if:

    a) $\frac{2}{3}$ = €86   b) $\frac{7}{8}$ = €133   c) $\frac{3}{10}$ = €192   d) $\frac{6}{7}$ = €144

    e) $\frac{5}{9}$ = €235   f) $\frac{9}{11}$ = €207   g) $\frac{8}{9}$ = €472   h) $\frac{11}{12}$ = €242

3. If Joe lost €24, which was $\frac{2}{5}$ of his money, when he went to the bowling alley, how much money had he to start with?

4. Tom had collected 258 stamps, but this was only $\frac{3}{8}$ of the amount that Bill had collected. How many stamps did Bill have?

Puzzler

A woman has a daughter who is $\frac{4}{9}$ of her age. If the daughter is 28 years old, what age is the mother? How long will it be before the daughter is exactly $\frac{1}{2}$ of her mother's age?

Express One Amount as a Fraction of Another

If a baker made 12 éclairs but only sold 9 of them, what fraction of the éclairs did he sell?

The numerator of the fraction will be the number that he sold = $\dfrac{9}{12}$
The denominator will be the total number of éclairs =

But you can reduce this fraction to its lowest terms by dividing by the HCF of 9 and 12.

$$\frac{9}{12} \div \frac{3}{3} = \frac{3}{4}$$

So to write one number as a fraction of another, we make the smaller number the numerator, we make the bigger number the denominator and we reduce to its lowest terms if we can.

5. What fraction is each of the following?

   a) 10c of 40c   b) 35cm of 50cm   c) €36 of €63   d) 49km of 84km

   e) 25 seconds of 1 minute   f) 56 of 96   g) 43 of 59

   h) 18 minutes of 1 hour

6. If a pizza was divided up into 16 slices and I ate 4 slices, what faction of the pizza is left?

7. If Mary had 72 marbles but she lost 32 of them, what fraction of her marbles has she lost?

8. If I had a party that 81 people attended but 27 of the guests got food poisoning, what fraction of the guests did not get food poisoning?

9. If a football team scored a total of 60 points out of a possible 96 over a league season, what fraction of the possible points did they get?

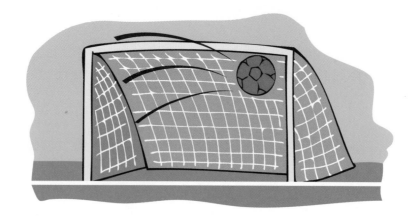

Homework

1. Change these mixed numbers into fractions.

   a) $1\frac{1}{3} = \frac{}{3}$

   b) $1\frac{4}{7} = \frac{}{7}$

   c) $1\frac{5}{6} = \frac{}{6}$

   d) $2\frac{2}{3} = \frac{}{3}$

   e) $2\frac{3}{5} = \frac{}{5}$

   f) $3\frac{1}{4} = \frac{}{4}$

   g) $3\frac{5}{8} = \frac{}{8}$

   h) $4\frac{1}{6} = \frac{}{6}$

   i) $3\frac{2}{9} = \frac{}{9}$

   j) $5\frac{1}{2} = \frac{}{2}$

   k) $6\frac{3}{4} = \frac{}{4}$

   l) $7\frac{4}{5} = \frac{}{5}$

2. Change these improper fractions to mixed numbers.

   a) $\frac{10}{7} =$

   b) $\frac{11}{6} =$

   c) $\frac{15}{8} =$

   d) $\frac{10}{3} =$

   e) $\frac{14}{5} =$

   f) $\frac{17}{4} =$

   g) $\frac{13}{9} =$

   h) $\frac{22}{5} =$

   i) $\frac{33}{10} =$

   j) $\frac{23}{2} =$

   k) $\frac{41}{11} =$

   l) $\frac{23}{6} =$

   m) $\frac{49}{8} =$

   n) $\frac{52}{7} =$

   o) $\frac{67}{12} =$

   p) $\frac{88}{9} =$

3. Fill in the missing numerators.

   a) $4 = \frac{}{4}$

   b) $8 = \frac{}{3}$

   c) $9 = \frac{}{6}$

   d) $5 = \frac{}{9}$

   e) $\frac{}{7} = 8$

   f) $\frac{}{8} = 9$

   g) $\frac{}{5} = 11$

   h) $\frac{}{12} = 7$

4. Add the following mixed numbers.
   a) $1\frac{3}{4} + 1\frac{2}{3}$
   b) $2\frac{1}{2} + 1\frac{7}{8}$
   c) $1\frac{2}{5} + 3\frac{1}{4}$
   d) $4\frac{1}{6} + 2\frac{1}{4}$
   e) $3\frac{5}{8} + 5\frac{7}{12}$
   f) $7\frac{1}{9} + 3\frac{5}{6}$

5. Find the difference between the following mixed numbers.
   a) $2\frac{2}{3} - 1\frac{1}{4}$
   b) $3\frac{7}{9} - 1\frac{1}{6}$
   c) $4\frac{7}{8} - 3\frac{5}{6}$
   d) $3\frac{3}{8} - 1\frac{1}{2}$
   e) $7\frac{1}{3} - 3\frac{3}{4}$
   f) $8\frac{1}{6} - 4\frac{5}{9}$

6. Find:
   a) $\frac{1}{5}$ of €275
   b) $\frac{1}{8}$ of €384
   c) $\frac{1}{6}$ of €504
   d) $\frac{1}{9}$ of €675
   e) $\frac{1}{4}$ of €2352
   f) $\frac{1}{7}$ of €2590

7. Find:
   a) $\frac{2}{3}$ of €876
   b) $\frac{3}{4}$ of €784
   c) $\frac{4}{5}$ of €1835
   d) $\frac{5}{6}$ of €1104
   e) $\frac{6}{7}$ of €1120
   f) $\frac{7}{8}$ of €3080

8. Work out the whole amount if:
   a) $\frac{2}{5} = €468$
   b) $\frac{3}{7} = €879$
   c) $\frac{4}{9} = €748$
   d) $\frac{5}{8} = €975$
   e) $\frac{7}{19} = €1372$
   f) $\frac{9}{11} = €1593$

9. What fraction is:
   a) 45 minutes of 1 hour
   b) 35cm of 1 metre
   c) €36 of €48
   d) 240g of 1kg
   e) 16 hours of 1 day
   f) 45 days of 1 year (not a leap year)

Recap

- I know how to change mixed numbers into improper fractions. ○ ○ ○
- I know how to change improper fractions into mixed numbers. ○ ○ ○
- I know how to write whole numbers as improper fractions. ○ ○ ○
- I can add mixed numbers. ○ ○ ○
- I can subtract mixed numbers. ○ ○ ○
- I can find a fraction of an amount. ○ ○ ○
- I can find the whole amount from a fraction. ○ ○ ○
- I can express one amount as a fraction of another. ○ ○ ○

18. Decimals

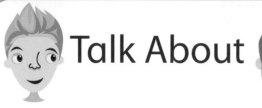 Talk About

Write Tenths as Decimals

This birthday cake has been divided into 10 slices of exactly the same size. There are marshmallows on 3 of the slices. We can write this as a fraction: $\frac{3}{10}$ of the slices have marshmallows. This can also be written as a decimal fraction.
Remember: the tenths come immediately after the decimal point, so $\frac{3}{10}$ is written as 0.3.

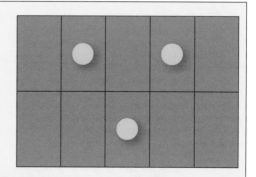

 Remember: $\frac{1}{10} = 0.1$ $\frac{3}{10} = 0.3$ $\frac{7}{10} = 0.7$

1. Change these fractions to decimal fractions.

   a) $\frac{2}{10}$ b) $\frac{8}{10}$ c) $\frac{6}{10}$ d) $\frac{4}{10}$

Mrs Green bought 2 of the cakes with the marshmallows on them for her son Greg's birthday. Greedy Greg ate 13 slices of cake by himself before going into sugar overload. So if each slice is $\frac{1}{10}$ of a cake, then Greg ate $\frac{13}{10}$. In other words, Greg ate 1 full cake and 3 slices, or $1\frac{3}{10}$.

We can write this as a decimal fraction by putting the units (number of full cakes he ate) on one side of the decimal point and the tenths (the number of extra slices he ate) on the other side of the decimal point.

$$1\frac{3}{10} = 1.3$$

The decimal point always separates the whole numbers from the fractions and it never moves.

2. Now write these improper fractions as decimal fractions. Don't forget to change them into mixed numbers first.

   a) $\frac{11}{10}$ b) $\frac{19}{10}$ c) $\frac{14}{10}$ d) $\frac{15}{10}$

   e) $\frac{23}{10}$ f) $\frac{30}{10}$ g) $\frac{37}{10}$ h) $\frac{41}{10}$

Strand: Number
Curriculum Objectives:
Compare and order fractions and decimals;
add and subtract decimals (to three decimal places) without and with a calculator;
multiply a decimal (up to three places) by a whole number, without and with a calculator;
divide a decimal number by a whole number, without and with a calculator;
solve problems involving decimals.

3. Change these decimals to fractions.
   a) 0.8
   b) 0.1
   c) 0.7
   d) 0.9
   e) 1.5
   f) 2.4
   g) 4.3
   h) 3.6

Write Hundredths as Decimals

John has 7c in his piggy bank. If there are 100c in €1, what fraction of a euro does he have in his piggy bank?

Well, he has 7 out of 100, so we can write it as $\frac{7}{100}$. The $\frac{1}{100}$s go beside the tenths after the decimal point, so $\frac{7}{100} = 0.07$.

4. Now try these.
   a) $3c = \frac{3}{100} = 0.03$
   b) $8c = \frac{8}{100} = 0.\underline{}$
   c) $9c = \frac{9}{100} = 0.\underline{}$
   d) $5c = \frac{5}{100} = 0.\underline{}$

What would happen if John had 18c in his piggy bank? How would we write it then?

Well, 18 out of 100 is $\frac{18}{100}$.

That is the same as $\frac{10}{100} + \frac{8}{100}$.

$\frac{10}{100}$ is the same as $\frac{1}{10}$, so $\frac{18}{100} = \frac{10}{100} + \frac{8}{100} = \frac{1}{10} + \frac{8}{100}$.

So we write $\frac{18}{100}$ as 0.18.

5. Now write these cent amounts as decimals. The first one has been done for you.
   a) $16c = \frac{16}{100} = \frac{1}{10} + \frac{6}{100} = 0.16$
   b) $12c = \frac{12}{100} =$
   c) $29c = \frac{29}{100} =$
   d) $35c = \frac{35}{100} =$
   e) $47c =$
   f) $53c =$

Remember: the decimal point separates the full euros from the cents.

If you have 139c in your pocket, you have 1 full euro and 39c, so we write it as €1.39.

6. Write these cent amounts as decimals with the euro sign.
   a) $178c = €\underline{}$
   b) $201c =$
   c) $376c =$
   d) $409c =$
   e) $520c =$
   f) $900c =$

Write the number represented by this notation board.

T	U	•	$\frac{1}{10}$	$\frac{1}{100}$
■ ■ ■ ■ ■	■ ■ ■			■ ■ ■ ■ ■ ■ ■

5 tens	+	3 units	+	0 tenths	+	7 hundredths
50	+	3	+	$\frac{0}{100}$	=	**53.07**

7. Now try this one.

T	U	•	$\frac{1}{10}$	$\frac{1}{100}$
■ ■ ■ ■	■ ■ ■ ■ ■		■	■ ■ ■

8. Write these as decimals.

   a) 3 hundreds + 2 tens + 4 units + 5 tenths + 1 hundredth = 324._____

   b) 1 hundred + 7 tens + 0 units + 3 tenths + 8 hundredths =

   c) 9 hundreds + 2 tens + 3 units + 0 tenths + 5 hundredths =

   d) 4 hundreds + 0 tens + 5 units + 7 tenths + 9 hundredths =

9. What does the digit 8 represent in each of the following numbers? Is it a hundred, ten, unit, tenth or hundredth?

   a) 512.8   b) 28.25   c) 2.38   d) 186.45   e) 876.5   f) 9.48

10. What digit in each of the following is a tenth and which is a hundredth?

   a) 327.96   b) 34.14   c) 10.05   d) 22.835

Write Thousandths as Decimals

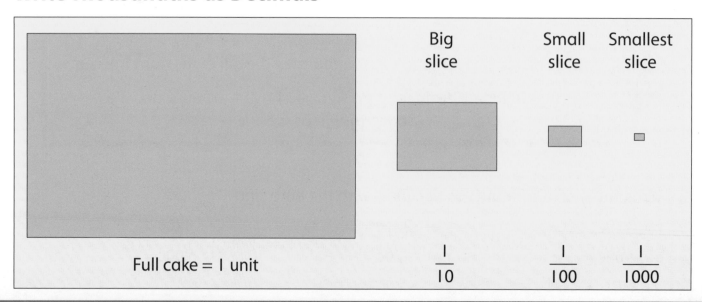

	Big slice	Small slice	Smallest slice
Full cake = 1 unit	$\frac{1}{10}$	$\frac{1}{100}$	$\frac{1}{1000}$

1. Stephen invited 9 of his friends to his birthday party. He had a large lemon cake and each person got a big slice. Have a look at the picture on the previous page and try to answer these questions.

   a) How many big slices make up the full cake?

   b) How many small slices are in each big slice?

   c) How many smallest slices are there in each small slice?

   d) How many smallest slices are in each big slice?

   e) How many smallest slices are in the full cake?

   f) Write a big slice and a small slice as a decimal fraction of the full cake.

If Stephen's cat, Dibbles, ate 8 smallest slices of the cake that fell on the floor, how much of the full cake had she eaten?

Well, we know that there are 1000 smallest slices in the full cake, so 8 smallest slices $= \frac{8}{1000}$

We can write this as a decimal fraction. The thousandths go beside the hundredths, so $\frac{8}{1000} = 0.008$

---

2. Write these as decimals.

   a) 5 smallest slices $= \frac{5}{1000} =$

   b) 1 smallest slice $= \frac{1}{1000} =$

   c) 9 smallest slices $= \frac{9}{1000} =$

   d) 7 smallest slices $=$

   e) 4 smallest slices $=$

   f) 8 smallest slices $=$

Terry the tortoise ate 56 of the smallest slices.

56 smallest slices $= \frac{56}{1000} = \frac{50}{1000} + \frac{6}{1000} = \frac{5}{100} + \frac{6}{1000} = 0.056$

Gerry the gerbil ate a whopping 195 smallest slices.

195 smallest slices $= \frac{195}{1000} = \frac{100}{1000} + \frac{90}{1000} + \frac{5}{1000} = \frac{1}{10} + \frac{9}{100} + \frac{5}{1000} = 0.195$

---

3. Now write these as decimals.

   a) 79 smallest slices $= \frac{79}{1000} =$

   b) 43 smallest slices $= \frac{43}{1000} =$

   c) 92 smallest slices $= \frac{92}{1000} =$

   d) 184 smallest slices $=$

   e) 267 smallest slices $=$

   f) 805 smallest slices $=$

4. What does the digit 5 in 22.835 represent? Try filling in the number on a notation board.

T	U	•	$\frac{1}{10}$	$\frac{1}{100}$	$\frac{1}{1000}$

5. Draw notation boards to represent the following numbers.

   a) 124.955   b) 613.419   c) 60.178

   d) 745.4   e) 29.632   f) 8.005

When measuring, we use the prefixes kilo and milli. Kilo means a thousand times bigger and milli means a thousand times smaller. If you look at your ruler, the smallest measurement is a millimetre, or mm.

Each mm = $\frac{1}{1000}$ of a metre, or 0.001m.

So 2mm = $\frac{2}{1000}$m = 0.00___m.

3mm = $\frac{3}{1000}$m = 0.00___m

6. Now write these lengths as decimals of a metre.

   a) 4mm   b) 7mm   c) 6mm   d) 9mm   e) 5mm

Kilo is used in the words kilogram (a thousand grams), kilometre (a thousand metres).

If we are measuring items smaller than a kg or km, we can use the decimal system.

1g = $\frac{1}{1000}$kg = 0.001kg   2m = $\frac{2}{1000}$km = 0.002km

7. Write these measurements as kg or km using the decimal system.

   a) 7g = 0.00___kg   b) 9m = 0.00___km   c) 24g

   d) 65g   e) 238m   f) 376m

   g) 237g   h) 978m   i) 6g

> **Task:** Find an object in your classroom that weighs 0.005kg.

8. Can you write these fractions as decimals?

   a) $\frac{2}{1000}$ b) $\frac{41}{1000}$ c) $\frac{323}{1000}$ d) $\frac{999}{1000}$ e) $\frac{417}{1000}$ f) $\frac{847}{1000}$

9. Now try these.

   a) $\frac{200}{1000}$ b) $\frac{450}{1000}$ c) $\frac{625}{1000}$ d) $\frac{60}{1000}$ e) $\frac{924}{1000}$ f) $\frac{4}{1000}$

10. What digit is in the thousandths place?

   a) 22.157   b) 8.915   c) 16.232

   d) 6.349   e) 2.307   f) 70.554

   g) 125.672   h) 214.816   i) 356.279

Write Other Fractions as Decimals

Sometimes the denominator is not a tenth, hundredth or thousandth, so it can be tricky turning it into a decimal fraction. For some, we can convert them to equivalent fractions in tenths or hundredths.

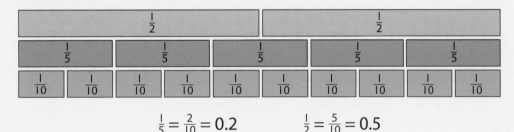

$$\frac{1}{5} = \frac{2}{10} = 0.2 \qquad \frac{1}{2} = \frac{5}{10} = 0.5$$

1. Now try these. Use the fraction wall above to help.

   a) $\frac{2}{5} = \frac{}{10} = 0.\_\_\_$ b) $\frac{4}{5}$ c) $\frac{3}{5}$

2. Can you fill in the missing numbers? Check your answers with the person beside you.

   a)
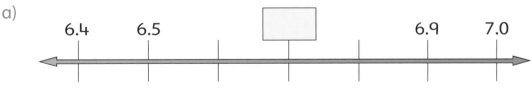

   b)

c)

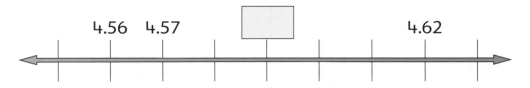

4.56 4.57   4.62

d)

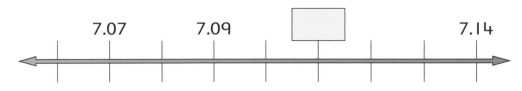

7.07   7.09   7.14

e)

1.253   1.259

f)

5.625 5.626   5.631

3. Draw some number lines to show the following numbers.

    a) 5.59   b) 2.679   c) 6.13   d) 12.4   e) 55.06   f) 10.375

On a number line, is 2.7 nearer to 2 or to 3?

1.9   2   2.7   3

It is nearer to 3, so 3 is the nearest whole number to 2.7.

When rounding decimals to the nearest whole unit, we need to look at the tenths. If it is less than five, we round down to the nearest whole unit. If it is five or more, we round up to the nearest whole unit.

---

4. Round these decimals to the nearest whole number.

    a) 7.9   b) 3.14   c) 14.2

    d) 28.99   e) 6.14   f) 9.8

    g) 126.11   h) 27.23   i) 20.06

5. Put the following decimals in order, starting with the lowest value.

    a) 5.2, 5.12, 5.016, 5.25, 5.78   b) 13.6, 13.47, 13.61, 13.655, 13

    c) 128.8, 128.42, 129, 128.97, 128.172   d) 1.573, 1.8, 1.57, 1.82, 1.753

    e) 425.2, 425.01, 425.001, 425.1, 425.25

Who cycled further?
Tom 12.804km
Carl 12.704km

Whose bag weighed more?
Ciara 3.145kg
Joan 3.154kg

6. Make a true statement by adding either <, > or = to each of the following.
(Hint: change them all to decimals first.)

a) 5.825 $5\frac{1}{10}$

b) $1\frac{7}{1000}$ 1.007

c) 23.5 $23\frac{61}{100}$

d) $180\frac{3}{10}$ 180.355

e) $8\frac{3}{100}$ 68.03

f) 470.765 $470\frac{4}{5}$

7. Continue these sequences.

a) 3.3, 3.4, 3.5, _____, _____, _____

b) 25.126, 25.127, 25.128, _____, _____, _____

c) 1.4, 1.6, 1.8, _____, _____, _____

d) 56.65, 56.7, 56.75, _____, _____, _____

e) 3.757, 3.756, 3.755, _____, _____, _____

f) State what is being either added or taken away in each case (for example, in part a), +0.1 is being added).

8. A butcher was weighing and packaging some chickens that had been delivered to the shop. Help her put them in order of weight, starting with the lightest, so that she can price them.

3.182kg, 1.907kg, 4.026kg, 1.669kg, 2.81kg, 3.1kg, 1.947kg

Puzzler
Can you complete this decimal magic square?

The magic number is 3.6.

1.4		
1.2		0.9

Adding Decimals

Eoin earned €8.85 mowing lawns and Sara earned €7.10 delivering leaflets. How much money do they have between them? Estimate to the nearest euro.

€8.85 to the nearest euro = €9
€7.10 to the nearest euro = €7
Therefore, €9 + €7 = €16

Now let's see if this was a good estimate by adding the 2 amounts of money that Eoin and Sara earned.

€ 8.85
€ 7.10
─────
€15.95

The golden rule when adding or subtracting decimals is to **make sure that the decimal points are always directly underneath each other.** That way, the tens are always under the tens, the units are under the units, the tenths are under the tenths and so on.

Kevin bought some groceries weighing 4.637kg, 21.4kg and 6.82kg and is about to cycle home on his bicycle. He has to put them in the basket on the bicycle and wants to know how heavy they are altogether. Can you help him?

Try this one: 4.637 + 21.4 + 6.82 =

```
    4.637
   21.4
+   6.82   kg
─────────
```

We can put in 0 as placeholders **after the number**, so our sum now looks like this:

```
    4.637
   21.400
+   6.820  kg
─────────
```

Have a go!

1. Work out these decimal additions. Remember to put the decimal points directly underneath each other and use 0s as placeholders.

   a) $6.78 + 12.45 + 1.2$
   b) $2.387 + 65.102$
   c) $7.9 + 31.12 + 2.51$
   d) $8.14 + 6.2 + 24.04$
   e) $135.8 + 2\frac{1}{10} + 7$
   f) $12.8 + 100.45 + 5\frac{1}{2}$

2. a) Emma's mum is out shopping and wants to find how heavy her bag will be. Add up the items for her.

   b) Find the total cost of her shopping too.

Subtracting Decimals

From a roll of silk material measuring 21.45m, Joan cuts a piece 6.3m long for a customer. How much material is left on the roll for Joan to sell?

When subtracting, we also need to subtract units from units, tenths from tenths, hundredths from hundredths and so on.

So 21.45 – 6.3 looks like:

$$
\begin{array}{r} 21.45 \\ -\ \ 6.3 \\ \hline \end{array}
\quad \text{or} \quad
\begin{array}{r} 21.45 \\ -\ \ 6.30 \\ \hline \end{array}
$$

Have a go!   m   m

3. Can you subtract these?

   a) $34.7 – 21.2$
   b) $88.04 – 50.8$
   c) $126.8 – 49.52$
   d) $56.45 – 18.39$
   e) $10.245 – 7.86$
   f) $436.879 – 125.6$
   g) $23.59 – 4.176$
   h) $22.734 – 9.615$
   i) $100 – 14.428$

4. Jan Zelezny of the Czech Republic is the current world record holder for the javelin. His longest throw of 98.48m was set in 1996. During his career he broke the world record for the javelin 5 times. On the next page is a list of those world record-breaking throws. Work out by what distance he improved his record each time and then work out the difference between the distances he threw for his first world record and the record that he still holds today.

Year	Distance
1987	87.66m
1990	89.66m
1993	95.54m
1993	95.66m
1996	98.48m

Multiplying Decimals

1. Try these on your calculator. What do you notice?

   a) 2.35×10

   b) 45.1×10

   c) 6.12×10

   d) 2.349×100

   e) 67.31×100

   f) 121.3×100

   g) 1.903×1000

   h) 3.588×1000

   i) 25.298×1000

> How would you describe what happens to the numbers when you multiply by 10, 100 and 1000?

2. Try these multiplication questions without using your calculator.

   a) 7.2×10

   b) 58.12×100

   c) 20.9×10

   d) 6.879×1000

   e) 10.09×10

   f) 0.25×100

   g) 3.2×100

   h) 4.7×1000

   i) 2.906×10

> James bought 2 large pizzas for his party. When working out the cost, he could add €14.65 + €14.65 or he could multiply €14.65 × 2.
>
> $$\begin{array}{r} €14.65 \\ \times \quad\quad 2 \\ \hline €29.30 \end{array}$$
>
> What do you notice about the decimal point in the answer?

3. Now try these. Remember to put in the decimal point.

   a) 7.21×6

   b) 45.08×4

   c) 2.639×8

   d) 134.7×5

   e) 78.09×2

   f) 16.25×3

   g) 1.49×9

   h) 5.702×7

   i) 0.98×8

4. Mr Powers's 5th class are going into Dublin City on a day trip. The DART ticket costs €1.34 return per child. There are 32 children in the class. What will the total bill for the children be?

(2 decimal places)

```
    1.34
  ×  32
   ─────
    268
   4020
```

(2 decimal places) ＿＿.＿＿ 42.88

a) Only 29 children will be coming on the day trip. Work out the total train bill now.

b) The class will be visiting a Viking exhibition with an entrance cost of €3.25 per child. Calculate the total bill for 29 children.

c) Lunch will be eaten in a restaurant @ €5.65 per person. How much will lunch cost for 29 children and 3 adults?

d) Calculate the total cost per child for the day.

5. Have a go. Check your answers with a calculator.
   a) 4.21 × 46
   b) 8.125 × 25
   c) 50.92 × 18
   d) 1.872 × 79
   e) 5.85 × 40
   f) 50.9 × 47

Dividing Decimals

Draw a line measuring 3.6cm with your ruler. Can you divide this line into 4 equal parts with your ruler? Now check your answer.

$$3.6 ÷ 4$$

```
4 | 3.6            or            4 | 3.6
  ─────                          ─────
  0.9                            0.9
```

1. Draw the following lines and divide each into 5 equal parts. First use your ruler and then check your answers, as above.
   a) 7.5cm
   b) 12.5cm
   c) 20.5cm
   d) 15cm

2. Divide:
   a) 4.8 ÷ 4
   b) 12.68 ÷ 2
   c) 9.125 ÷ 5
   d) 47.34 ÷ 9
   e) 59.88 ÷ 6
   f) 863.1 ÷ 7
   g) 2.52 ÷ 18
   h) 92.5 ÷ 25
   i) 9.92 ÷ 31

3. Divide the following decimals by 10, 100 and 1000 using your calculator. Record your results in the table.

	÷ 10	÷ 100	÷ 1000
34.65			
168.2			
3.795			
1258.6			
540.01			
28.42			
189.7			

Can you come up with a rule for dividing by 10, 100 and 1000 from your results?

4. Using your rule, divide the following.

a) $3.9 \div 10$

b) $21.88 \div 100$

c) $612.5 \div 100$

d) $502.5 \div 1000$

e) $99.2 \div 10$

f) $96.8 \div 10$

g) $313.17 \div 100$

h) $62.54 \div 1000$

i) $1.275 \div 100$

Calculating Decimals

$$\frac{1}{5} = \frac{2}{10} = 0.2$$

Using your calculator, can you find what $\frac{1}{5}$ is as a decimal without changing it to tenths? (Hint: use only the 1, 5, ÷ keys.)

Define your rule: To change a fraction into a decimal, divide the _____ into the

_____.

1. Try the same formula to change these fractions to decimals.

a) $\frac{1}{4}$

b) $\frac{7}{8}$

c) $\frac{3}{4}$

d) $\frac{4}{5}$

e) $\frac{3}{8}$

f) $\frac{5}{8}$

g) $\frac{3}{5}$

Homework

1. Change these fractions to decimal fractions.

   a) $\frac{7}{10}$ b) $\frac{5}{10}$ c) $\frac{9}{10}$ d) $\frac{3}{10}$

   e) $\frac{16}{10}$ f) $\frac{24}{10}$ g) $\frac{32}{10}$ h) $\frac{48}{10}$

2. Change these decimals to fractions.

   a) 0.6   b) 0.3   c) 0.4   d) 0.8

   e) 1.7   f) 5.1   g) 8.7   h) 9.9

3. Draw these numbers on notation boards.

   a) 21.05   b) 30.57   c) 3.91   d) 83.4

   e) 17.64   f) 40.08

4. Change these fractions to decimal fractions.

   a) $\frac{6}{100}$ b) $\frac{7}{100}$ c) $\frac{11}{100}$ d) $\frac{23}{100}$

   e) $\frac{18}{100}$ f) $\frac{37}{100}$ g) $\frac{85}{100}$ h) $\frac{90}{100}$

5. What is the value of the underlined digit in each of these numbers?

   a) 34.9<u>1</u>   b) 2<u>5</u>.08   c) 19.<u>7</u>3

   d) <u>6</u>9.2   e) 9<u>4</u>.89   f) 55.5<u>5</u>

6. Write these decimals as fractions.

   a) 0.007   b) 0.009   c) 0.017

   d) 0.079   e) 0.183   f) 0.431

7. What digit is in the thousandths place?

   a) 41.238   b) 9.134   c) 0.326

   d) 25.107   e) 314.133   f) 90.562

8. Round these decimals to the nearest whole number.

   a) 1.8   b) 9.3   c) 15.5

   d) 26.12   e) 46.89   f) 7.09

   g) 45.768   h) 2.144   i) 18.503

9. Put the following decimals in order, starting with the lowest value.

   a) 7.04, 7.4, 7.14, 7.145

   b) 12.034, 12.304, 12.34, 12.403

   c) 71.2, 71.19, 72.01, 71.21

   d) 0.872, 0.827, 0.278, 0.728

10. a) 17.1 + 2.75 + 29.804   b) 4.97 + 68.033 + 209.5   c) 0.774 + 81.92 + 2.6

    d) 612.234 + 4.01 + 34.47   e) 34.65 + 1.987 + 2.76   f) 6.902 + 0.41 + 27.8

11. a) 2.27 – 1.9   b) 65.03 – 25.845   c) 342.7 – 86.39

    d) 40.09 – 7.495   e) 8.201 – 3.54   f) 73.132 – 65.819

12. a) 1.83 × 9   b) 24.07 × 8   c) 6.814 × 7

    d) 58.06 × 14   e) 49.581 × 24   f) 1.675 × 37

13. a) 0.208 ÷ 8   b) 10.15 ÷ 7   c) 524.7 ÷ 9

    d) 75.6 ÷ 14   e) 24.03 ÷ 27   f) 86.4 ÷ 32

Recap

- I can write tenths as decimals. ○ ○ ○

- I can write hundredths as decimals. ○ ○ ○

- I can write thousandths as decimals. ○ ○ ○

- I can add decimals. ○ ○ ○

- I can subtract decimals. ○ ○ ○

- I can multiply decimals. ○ ○ ○

- I can divide decimals. ○ ○ ○

19. Money

 Talk About

1. a) List 5 countries that have the euro as their currency.
    b) What are the advantages of countries having the same currency?
    c) Name 3 countries that don't have the euro as their currency.
    d) What's the name of the currency in each of those countries?
    e) If you were going on holidays to one of those countries, what could be confusing about their currency?

2. Find out what a bureau de change is in a bank.

3. Find the individual price for each item from the following clues.
    a) If 4 games cost €108, how much do they each cost?
    b) I had €35. I bought 2 CDs and got €3.02 change. How much did 1 CD cost?
    c) If I download 8 songs onto my MP3 player and it cost me €3.12, how much did each song cost?
    d) I got 75c change from €62 when I bought 5 DVDs. How much did 1 DVD cost?

Value for Money

4. Let's see if we can get some better value. Which of these is better value?
    a) A banana costing 15c or a banana costing 18c
    b) 2 pencils costing 62c or 2 pencils costing 60c. How much do each of the pencils cost?

Strand: Measures
Curriculum Objectives:
Compare 'value for money' using unitary method.

133

Which is better value?

   a) 5 oranges for 80c   or   b) 4 oranges for 68c

To find out which is better value, we need to find the price of 1 orange in both cases.
This is called the **unitary method**, or finding 1 unit.

   a) 5 oranges = 80c   b) 4 oranges = 68c
       1 orange = 80 ÷ 5   1 orange = 68 ÷ 4
       1 orange = 16c   1 orange = 17c

5. Try using the unitary method in the following table to find whether A or B is better
    value.

A	B	Better Value: A or B?
5 apples for 90c	4 apples for 80c	
3 pens for €1.20	8 pens for €2.80	
7 bars for €1.75	10 bars for €2.20	

6. Jack would like to buy some goldfish and has been given these prices. Which option is
    better value?

   a)

5 for €30

   b)

3 for €15

Calculating Shopping Bills

Bill's Barbecue

Bill is having a barbecue at the weekend and has a lot to organise. Help him with his
shopping. (Hint: use the unitary method to find the value of 1 item and then multiply
by the number of items Bill wants.)

For example: 5 loaves of bread cost €4.45. How much will 7 loaves cost?

$$5 = €4.45$$
$$1 = €4.45 ÷ 5 = €0.89$$
$$7 = €0.89 × 7 = €6.23$$

1. Drinks
   a) 4 bottles of lemonade cost €5.60. How much will 10 bottles cost?
   b) 5 bottles of cola cost €8.00. How much will 8 bottles cost?
   c) 2 cartons of orange juice cost €3.10. Find the cost of 11 cartons of orange juice.
   d) If Bill buys 2 bottles of sparkling water @ €1.20 each, he will get the third bottle at half price. How much will he pay for the 3 bottles?
   e) The cost of 3 bottles of blackcurrant cordial is €5.85. What is the cost of 2 bottles?
   f) Calculate the total drinks bill.

2. Food
   a) 1 packet of 8 beef burgers costs €2.60. Find the cost of 3 packets.
   b) 10 sausages cost €1.99. How much will 40 sausages cost?
   c) 2 bags of thick-cut chips cost €4.60. Find the cost for 5 bags of chips.
   d) If Bill buys 2 bags of crisps @ €1.87 each, he will get the third bag free. How much will he pay for the 3 bags?
   e) If 3 bags of chicken nuggets cost €8.97, how much will 4 bags cost?
   f) 2 packs of hamburger buns cost €3.00. Find the cost of 3 bags.
   g) Ice cream costs €1.90 per litre tub. Find the cost of 5 litres.
   h) Calculate the total food bill.

3. Bill was trying to get value for his money by buying special offer products, such as buy two get the third free. List any other offers like this that you have seen while shopping.

4. Food items are usually sold by weight. Find 5 items that weigh the same amount and compare the prices. Which item is the best value?

Betty's Boutique

Monday	09:00 – 18:00
Tuesday	09:00 – 18:00
Wednesday	09:00 – 18:00
Thursday	09:00 – 18:00
Friday	09:00 – 18:00
Saturday	09:00 – 18:00

Calculating Wages

1. The clothes shop is open each week for the times listed on page 135. Marianne works in the shop every Saturday and earns €8.00 per hour. How much money does she earn each Saturday?

2. Kevin works in the shop on Mondays, Wednesdays and Fridays at €10.00 per hour. How much does he earn each week?

3. Joan works in the shop every day of the week and earns €96 per day. How much does she earn per hour, taking into consideration that she takes a 1-hour lunch break every day for which she isn't paid?

4. If there are 5 assistants, including Joan, who work the full week and each gets €96 per day, how much do they each earn per week?

5. What is the wage bill for these 5 assistants each week?

6. Andrew was offered a weekend job delivering newspapers for €20 per day. How long will it take him to save up for a €200 bicycle if he works both Saturday and Sunday every weekend?

7. Rachel has accepted a job to work for 9 hours each Saturday in a newsagent and has been given the following pay options: €72 per day or €8.25 per hour. Which option gives a better return for Rachel's work?

8. Here is a breakdown of the wages given in a factory. Each person works for 8 hours a day and 5 days a week. Complete the table.

Rate	Wages per Hour (€)	Wages per Day (€)	Wages per Week (€)
A	€10.60		
B			€480.00

Puzzler

3 workers each get paid depending on how many hours they have worked. Peter the carpenter worked for 3 times as long as Robbie the painter and Robbie worked 4 times as long as Thomas the electrician. The total wage bill was €510. How much was each person paid?

---

9. A teacher bought 32 English books @ €15.99 each and 32 science books @ €21.99 each. What was the total amount of money she had to pay for all the books?

10. If 4 new cars of the same make and model cost €88000, find the price of 1 of these cars.

11. Here are the prices for the Ryans' 2-week holiday to Portugal: 2 adults @ €899 each and 3 children @ €399. Calculate the total holiday price.

12. If a shopkeeper spent €2475.00 on 45 identical dresses, how much did each dress cost?

13. Work out this office manager's shopping bill with your calculator.

Item	Price
5 computers @ €799 each	
2 printers @ €99 each	
8 desks @ €299 each	
8 chairs @ €178 for 2	
1 fax machine @ €120 each	
2 filing cabinets @ €135.99 each	
10 boxes of paper @ €60 for 5	

Total:

14. Use your calculator to work out these wage bills.
   a) There are 250 bank workers who each earn an hourly rate of €18.50. If each person works a 40-hour week, calculate the total wage bill per week for the bank.
   b) A sales assistant earns a daily wage of €105.50. If he works 5 days a week and can take 2 weeks paid holiday a year, calculate his total yearly wage.

Homework

1. Jack went shopping and bought 7 of each of the following products for the prices shown in the table. When Jill went shopping she bought exactly the same products but she only bought 4 of each. Work out what she paid for each product.

Product	Jack (7)	Jill (4)
Pears	€3.92	
Packets of pasta	€9.66	
Yoghurts	€4.48	
Bottles of vinegar	€8.75	
Plums	€2.73	
Doughnuts	€5.04	

2. My true love went shopping and bought 5 gold rings @ €89 each, 4 calling birds @ €23.50 each, 3 French hens @ €17 each, 2 turtle doves @ €47.50 each and a partridge for €38. How much change did my true love get out of €800?

3. Work out the weekly wages of the following people. Can you work out the hidden mystery word?

Name	Hourly Pay	Hours Worked per Day	Days Worked per Week	Weekly Wage
Susan	€9	5	6	
Alan	€8.50	6	4	
Lauren	€13	4	7	
Ahmed	€9.40	8	3	
Rory	€11.80	7	5	
Yvonne	€16	9	2	

4. Fill in the blanks in the following table.

Name	Hourly Pay	Hours Worked per Day	Days Worked per Week	Weekly Wage
Patrick		8	3	€216
Amber	€8.50		4	€238
Yolanda	€14.00	3		€252

Recap

- I can calculate value for money. ○ ○ ○
- I can calculate shopping bills. ○ ○ ○
- I can calculate wages. ○ ○ ○

20. Rules and Properties

 **Talk About**

$7 + 6 + 9 =$	Now try this one.
What answer did you get? Which 2 numbers did you add first? How many different ways could you have done this sum? Would it make any difference to the final answer?	$15 - 7 - 6 =$ What answer did you get? Discuss your answer with the people near you. Did anyone get a different answer to you? How many possible answers are there? What are they?

1. Try these. See if they have more than 1 possible answer. If they do have more than 1 possible answer, work out each of the possibilities.

   a) $9 + 5 + 12$ b) $10 + 7 - 5$ c) $16 - 8 + 3$ d) $23 - 7 - 4$

   e) $3 \times 4 + 2$ f) $7 + 5 \times 3$ g) $5 \times 6 - 2$ h) $14 - 3 \times 3$

   i) $6 \times 2 \times 5$ j) $40 \div 5 + 3$ k) $30 + 6 \div 3$ l) $45 - 9 \div 3$

   m) $72 \div 12 - 4$ n) $60 \div 6 \times 2$ o) $9 \times 12 \div 4$ p) $24 \div 6 \div 2$

Do the Work Inside Brackets First

To help us find the particular answer that is being looked for, brackets are sometimes placed around 1 of the operations. We always perform the operation that is inside the brackets first.

$$23 - 9 + 4$$

Possibilities:

$(23 - 9) + 4 =$

   $14 \quad + 4 = 18$

$23 - (9 + 4) =$

   $23 - \quad 13 \quad = 10$

Strand: Algebra
Curriculum Objectives:
Explore and discuss simple properties and rules about brackets and priority of operation; identify relationships and record verbal and simple symbolic rules for number patterns.

1. Now try these. Record the different stages involved.
   a) $(24 + 17) - 9$
   b) $38 + (26 - 18)$
   c) $82 - (38 + 35)$
   d) $(35 - 18) + 97$
   e) $19 + (35 + 24)$
   f) $(12 \times 3) + 5$
   g) $7 \times (9 + 15)$
   h) $(27 + 16) \times 3$
   i) $49 + (8 \times 7)$
   j) $(9 \times 12) - 65$
   k) $11 \times (81 - 69)$
   l) $(25 - 19) \times 42$
   m) $87 - (9 \times 6)$
   n) $(83 - 32) - 18$
   o) $97 - (67 - 49)$

2. Now try these, either by doing the part in the brackets first, in your head or in a rough work column.
   a) $(9 \times 6) \times 8$
   b) $12 \times (9 \times 7)$
   c) $(29 + 25) \div 6$
   d) $47 + (96 \div 8)$
   e) $132 \div (6 + 5)$
   f) $(54 \div 6) + 73$
   g) $(108 - 59) \div 7$
   h) $104 - (36 \div 9)$
   i) $72 \div (51 - 39)$
   j) $(108 \div 9) - 7$
   k) $(21 \times 3) \div 9$
   l) $38 \times (28 \div 4)$
   m) $81 \div (3 \times 3)$
   n) $(42 \div 7) \times 78$
   o) $(144 \div 12) \div 3$
   p) $63 \div (45 \div 5)$

3. Use your calculator to work out the following.
   a) $(196 \times 46) + 3625$
   b) $(4982 + 1373) - 2548$
   c) $(414 \div 18) \times 74$
   d) $(54 \times 36) \div 9$
   e) $1005 - (436 \div 4)$
   f) $(2093 + 257) \div 5$

BODMAS

When there are no brackets, we perform the operations in this order of priority: division, multiplication, addition and finally subtraction.

A good way to remember the order is BODMAS:

Brackets **O**f **D**ivision **M**ultiplication **A**ddition **S**ubtraction

Check out *The BODMAS Song* on YouTube at www.youtube.com.

$39 + 12 \times 5 =$

We must multiply before we add, so
$39 + 60 = 99$

4. Now try these.
   a) 73 – 28 ÷ 4
   b) 81 ÷ 9 + 75
   c) 6 × 11 + 47
   d) 47 × 15 – 138
   e) 346 + 23 × 19
   f) 189 + 945 ÷ 7
   g) 1235 – 37 × 24
   h) 348 ÷ 6 – 27
   i) 435 + 189 – 256
   j) 58 × 96 ÷ 12
   k) 782 – 217 + 486
   l) 132 ÷ 11 × 78

5. Use your calculator to work these out.
   a) 2482 + 7985 – 6319
   b) 8327 – 76 × 48
   c) 138 × 46 + 3808
   d) 2544 ÷ 16 + 2846
   e) 2014 – 8456 ÷ 28
   f) 224 + 1904 ÷ 7

Puzzler

Put 4 coins in a row on a table, all tails up.
Turn any 3 coins over – this counts as 1 move.
You must turn 3 different coins to complete 1 move!
How many moves will it take to get all the coins on heads?

Patterns

1. Study this simple pattern. How would you describe the pattern to someone who could not see it? Try it with the people near you. What are the different elements? (Hint: colour / shape / size.)

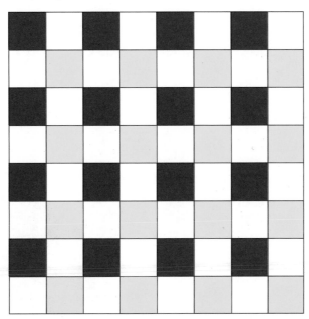

2. Using the squared pages in your maths copy, design some patterns of your own without letting the people near you see. Now pick 1 of your designs and describe it to the others. See if they can copy your design from your description. Try it out on each other.

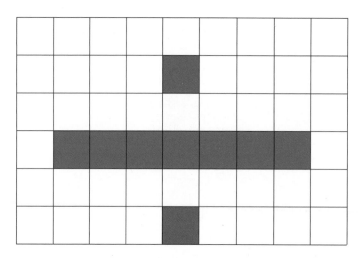

3. Draw some symbols yourself by creating patterns with the squares. Again, try them out on the people near you to see if they can guess what symbol you're describing.

4. You can also make letters and numbers from patterns of squares.

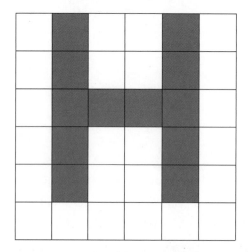

Try some of your own. You could even make words or messages.

5. We can also make patterns using only numbers.
   Look at this number pattern or sequence:

   1, 4, 7, 10, 13, 16

   What are the different elements of the pattern?
   (Hint: start / operation / number of terms.)

6. Now make these patterns.

    a) Start with the number 2. To find the next term, add 4. Each new term is 4 more than the previous term. There are 8 terms in the pattern.

    b) Start with the number 47. To find the next term, subtract 6. Each new term is 6 less than the previous term. There are 5 terms in the pattern.

    c) Start with the number 3. To find the next term, multiply by 3. Each new term is 3 times bigger than the previous term. There are 7 terms in the pattern.

    d) Start with the number 96. To find the next term, divide by 2. Each new term is half of the previous term. There are 6 terms in the pattern.

Recognise Patterns in Number Sequences

Look at these patterns. Write out how the sequence is extended.

1, 2, 4, 8, 16, 32   The sequence increases by (operation) by (number).
324, 108, 36, 12, 4   The sequence decreases by (operation) by (number).

1. Now try these. In each case, write out how the sequence is extended.

    a) 1, 5, 9, 13, 17, 21, 25   b) 78, 65, 52, 39, 26, 13

    c) 5, 10, 20, 40, 80, 160   d) 16, 44, 72, 100, 128, 156

    e) 625, 125, 25, 5, 1   f) 243, 81, 27, 9, 3, 1

    g) 72, 63, 54, 45, 36, 27, 18   h) 2, 12, 72, 432, 2592

2. In the following patterns, see if you can spot which term is the odd term out. You must be able to explain why it's the odd one out. Strictly no chancing your arm!

    a) 3, 10, 17, 25, 31, 38, 45

    b) 9, 18, 36, 72, 144, 248

    c) 95, 79, 63, 48, 31, 15

    d) 512, 256, 128, 64, 31, 16, 8, 4, 2, 1

3. In these patterns, the last 3 terms have been left for you to fill in.

    a) 14, 33, 52, 71, ___, ___, ___   b) 107, 92, 77, 62, ___, ___, ___

    c) 2, 6, 18, 54, ___, ___, ___   d) 96, 48, 24, ___, ___, ___

Extending Number Sequences

It can sometimes be trickier to spot how a sequence is being extended.
Look at this pattern:

$$1, 2, 4, 7, 11, 16, 22$$

What is happening each time?

4. Now fill in the missing terms in these patterns.

a) 1, 2, 5, 10, 17, ___, ___, ___

b) 34, 33, 31, 28, ___, ___, ___

c) 3, 13, 21, 27, ___, ___, ___

d) 1, 3, 6, 10, ___, ___, ___

e) 70, 57, 46, 37, ___, ___, ___

f) 10, 70, 120, 160, ___, ___, ___

g) 1, 5, 4, 8, 7, 11, ___, ___, ___

h) 42, 36, 38, 32, 34, ___, ___, ___

Can You Crack the Code to the Safe?

5. This is the keypad on a safe. To open the safe, you must press each of the buttons once but in the right order. You must get the sequence right. The first number is a single-digit number. The next number in the sequence is found by adding, subtracting, multiplying or dividing by 3. You do the same for the rest of the terms in the sequence.

27	11	6
8	14	39
42	9	24

Who will be the first to crack the code? Your time starts now!

___, ___, ___, ___, ___, ___, ___, ___, ___

6. Now try this one. The first number in the sequence is a 2-digit number. You find each remaining term by adding, subtracting multiplying or dividing by 5. What is the code?

10	8	35
12	15	40
3	7	50

___, ___, ___, ___, ___, ___, ___, ___, ___

7. Make up your own codes and try them out on the people near you. Work out the sequence first yourself. Be careful how you arrange the numbers on the keypad.

Homework

1. Try these. See if they have more than 1 possible answer. If they do have more than 1 possible answer, work out each of the possibilities.

a) $6 + 8 + 9$

b) $14 + 9 - 2$

c) $19 - 4 + 7$

d) $26 - 9 - 8$

e) $6 \times 2 + 5$

f) $4 + 8 \times 6$

g) $2 \times 9 - 7$

h) $11 - 4 \times 2$

i) $3 \times 3 \times 9$

j) $36 \div 3 + 3$

k) $24 + 8 \div 4$

l) $39 - 3 \div 3$

2. Now try these.

   a) (45 + 36) − 29   b) 54 + (32 − 17)   c) 75 − (28 + 16)   d) 9 × (14 + 12)

   e) (19 + 32) × 5   f) 37 + (9 × 6)   g) 91 − (7 × 7)   h) (65 − 28) − 29

   i) 88 − (73 − 35)   j) (113 − 49) ÷ 8   k) 92 − (42 ÷ 6)   l) 81 ÷ (38 − 29)

3. Use your calculator to work these out.

   a) (27 × 125) + 1483   b) (3177 + 1908) − 4225   c) (437 ÷ 23) × 59

   d) (37 × 42) ÷ 6   e) 2127 − (245 ÷ 5)   f) (6185 + 794) ÷ 7

4. Can you spot the pattern?

   a) 2, 6, 10, 14, 18, 22, 26   b) 63, 56, 49, 42, 35, 28   c) 1, 5, 10, 16, 23, 31

   d) 3, 9, 27, 81, 243, 729   e) 96, 48, 24, 12, 6   f) 5, 11, 8, 14, 11, 17

5. Work out the patterns and fill in the missing terms.

   a) 8, 16, 24, 32, ___, ___, ___   b) 81, 70, 60, 51, ___, ___, ___

   c) 1, 4, 9, 16, 25, ___, ___, ___   d) 20, 10, 50, 40, 80, ___, ___, ___

   e) 3, 7, 13, 21, 31, ___, ___, ___   f) 55, 48, 51, 44, 47, ___, ___, ___

Recap

- I know to do the work inside the brackets first.

- I know what BODMAS means.

- I can recognise and describe patterns.

- I can recognise patterns in number sequences.

- I can extend number sequences.

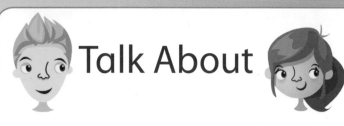

Talk About

1. Count how many steps it takes you to walk from the classroom to the office. Write it down. When you get back to the classroom, compare your answers with your friends' answers.

    a) What do you notice?

    b) Who is right?

    c) What's the problem?

    d) What do we need?

    e) What instrument could we use to measure the distance accurately?

Fred used a metre stick to measure the height of his friend, Frank. He measured Frank as being 1m and 57cm tall. But how many centimetres tall is he?

$$1m = 100cm$$

So 1m 57cm = 100cm + 57cm = 157cm

But if there are 100cm in 1 metre, what fraction of a metre is 1cm?

$$1cm = \frac{1}{100}m$$

Now write it as a decimal.

$$1cm = 0.01m$$

So Frank is 1m 57cm = 157cm = $1\frac{57}{100}$m = 1.57m tall.

Strand: Measures
Curriculum Objectives:
Select and use appropriate instruments of measurement;
estimate and measure length using appropriate metric units;
estimate and measure the perimeter of regular and irregular shapes.

2. Fill in the blanks.

a) 1m 35cm = _____cm

b) 243cm = _____m _____cm

c) $3\frac{3}{4}$m = _____cm

d) 2.17m = _____m _____cm

e) 5m 91cm = _____m

f) 3m 5cm = _____m

g) $1\frac{9}{100}$m = _____m _____cm

h) $7\frac{3}{10}$m = _____m

3. a) Julie has to walk 1km 234m to school every day. How far does she walk in metres?

b) What fraction of 1 kilometre is 1 metre? Remember: 1000m = 1km.

c) How far does Julie walk in km? Write it as a mixed number and a decimal.

4. Now try these.

a) 3984m = _____km _____m

b) 1km 98m = _____m

c) 1.238km = _____m

d) 435m = _____km

e) $2\frac{132}{1000}$km = _____m

f) $8\frac{19}{1000}$km = _____km

g) $6\frac{9}{10}$km = _____km _____m

h) 10km 73m = _____km

Adding and Subtracting Metres and Centimetres

In a long jump competition, John jumped a distance of 4m 78cm in the first round, 5.09m in the second round and 486cm in the third round. What was the total distance John jumped in the competition?

When you add lengths, each of the lengths must be written the same way. So here we have 3 possibilities.

cm	m	cm	m
478	4	78	4.78
509	5	9	5.09
+ 486	+ 4	86	+ 4.86

Check to see that the answers are the same in each case.

1. Now try these. You can choose whichever way you prefer, but it is very important that you record the unit of measurement in your answer. For example, is it 3.75 metres or 3.75 crocodiles? If you don't say, we won't know.

   a) 1m 34cm + 257cm + 4.92m

   b) 538cm + 7m 6cm + 8.49m

   c) $2\frac{1}{2}$m + 73cm + 9.81m

   d) 4m 56cm + 3.07m

   e) $3\frac{1}{4}$m + 496cm + $1\frac{1}{5}$m

   f) 2.48m + $1\frac{9}{10}$m + 38cm

   g) 6m 85cm + 903cm + 2.26m

   h) $3\frac{3}{5}$m + 5.53m + 10m 74cm

   > We have the same choices when we are subtracting.

2. Sheila's didgeridoo is 2.87m long. Bruce's didgeridoo is 195cm long. How much longer is Sheila's didgeridoo?

3. Now try these.

   a) 7m 27cm – 148cm

   b) 8.03m – 5m 45cm

   c) 936cm – 3.79m

   d) 6m 4cm – 4.95m

   e) 1m 53cm – 86cm

   f) $8\frac{7}{100}$m – 3m 29cm

   g) 4.16m – $2\frac{4}{5}$m

   h) 563cm – 1m 84cm

Adding and Subtracting Kilometres and Metres

We have similar choices when we add or subtract kilometres and metres.

If the shopping centre is 2km 38m from your house and the cinema is only 1.65km from your house, how much nearer is the cinema than the shopping centre?

m		km	m		km
2038		2	38		2.038
– 1650		– 1	650		–1.650

4. Now try these.

   a) 2km 347m + 849m + 6.174km

   b) $1\frac{78}{1000}$km + 5km 26m + 9483m

   c) 7.73km + $2\frac{1}{8}$km + 6km 239m

   d) 5km 7m + 2.3km + $3\frac{3}{4}$km

   e) 9km 27m – 1.635km

   f) 4716m – 3km 248m

   g) 7.042km – 385m

   h) $6\frac{5}{8}$km – 4km 8m

5. A man set a world record for walking while balancing an ice cream cone on his nose. He managed to walk a distance of 1km 437m before the cone fell off. The following year, after intensive training, he increased his world record to 2km 76m. How much further had he walked to set the new world record?

6. If you walked 1km 459m to the shops, a further 962m to the library and then 1.284km to get back home, how far would you have walked altogether?

7. Setting out from his favourite spot in the garden at 8:00am, a snail travelled a distance of 1.39m in the first hour, 1m 6cm in the second hour and 153cm in the third hour. How far had the snail travelled by 11:00am?

8. From a piece of wood measuring 8m 42cm, a piece 2.79m long was cut off. What was the length of the remaining piece of wood?

Write cm as mm and Vice Versa

How many centimetres long is this line? _____

What problem do we have in measuring it?

When we are measuring smaller objects, we need a smaller unit of measurement. Look at your ruler. Look at the space between the 0 and 1cm lines. That space has been divided up into 10 smaller spaces. Each of these smaller spaces measures **1 millimetre (mm)**. There are 10 millimetres in a centimetre **(10mm = 1cm)**.

The first part of the word millimetre (milli) refers to 1000, just like millennium refers to a thousand years. This suggests that there are 1000 millimetres in a metre. Let's see if that's right.

There are 10 millimetres in 1 centimetre.

There are 100 centimetres in 1 metre.   So 10 × 100 = 1000.

1. Draw 5 lines of different lengths in your copy. Now swap copies with the person beside you and estimate how long their lines are. Then measure their 5 lines to see how close your estimates are. Record your answers in centimetres and millimetres.

2. Now measure the lengths of these lines.

_____   _____

_____   _____

_____   _____

3. Estimate the lengths of these lines. Measure them afterwards to see how close your estimate was.

_____   _____

_____   _____

_____   _____

Remember: an estimate can't be right or wrong, but some estimates are better than others.

Pat measured the thickness of his dictionary and found it to be 2.7cm thick. How many millimetres thick is the dictionary?

$2.7\text{cm} = 2\frac{7}{10}\text{cm}$

But because there are only 10mm in 1cm, then $\frac{7}{10}\text{cm} = 7\text{mm}$.

So $2\frac{7}{10}\text{cm} = 2\text{cm } 7\text{mm} = 27\text{mm}$.

4. Fill in the blanks.

   a) 13mm = ____cm ____mm   b) 5cm 3mm = ____cm   c) 8.1cm = ____mm

   d) 3cm 8mm = ____mm   e) 104mm = ____cm ____mm f) ____cm = 12cm 5mm

   g) $9\frac{3}{10}$cm = ____mm   h) ___cm ____mm = $5\frac{1}{2}$cm   i) $8\frac{3}{5}$cm = ____cm

5. Now try these.

   a) 3cm 5mm + 28mm + 5.7cm   b) 92mm + $7\frac{4}{5}$cm + 6cm 8mm

   c) 109mm + 8.8cm + $12\frac{3}{10}$cm   d) $7\frac{1}{2}$cm + 3cm 9mm + 5.4cm

   e) 9cm 2mm – 58mm   f) 119mm – 5.4cm

   g) 8.2cm – 4cm 8mm   h) 12cm 5mm – 108mm

6. Jim's pencil is 4cm 3mm long. Lisa's pencil is 8.6cm long. Bill's pencil is 148mm long.

    a) What is the difference in length between Bill and Lisa's pencil?

    b) What is the combined length of Jim and Bill's pencils?

    c) Lisa uses her pencil a lot. After paring it and using it for a few days, the length of her pencil had decreased by 3cm 9mm. What length is her pencil now?

    d) Bill's pencil has decreased by 1.3cm and Jim's pencil has decreased by 17mm. What is the total length of the 3 pencils now?

Multiplying and Dividing Lengths

Anne needs to repair the fence in her back garden. She needs 7 pieces of wood exactly 1m 4cm long. What is the total length of timber she needs?

The quickest way to work this out is to multiply. Just like when we were adding and subtracting lengths, we have choices.

cm			m	cm			m	
104			1	04			1.04	
× 7			×	7			× 7	

Choose which way you prefer.

We have the same choices when we are dividing.

1. If the wood cost €3 per metre, how much did Anne have to pay?

Choose whichever way you prefer and work out the answers to the following questions. Remember to record the unit of measurement in your answer.

2. a) 4m 27cm × 8   b) 209cm × 6   c) 5.74m × 9

    d) 3km 42m × 5   e) 9.146km × 4   f) 7053m × 7

    g) 39mm × 12   h) 7cm 9mm × 3   i) 4.8cm × 11

3. Now try these.

a) 156mm ÷ 4

b) 2km 344m ÷ 8

c) 11.76m ÷ 7

d) 5m 4cm ÷ 12

e) 56.7cm ÷ 9

f) 3975m ÷ 5

g) 9.053km ÷ 11

h) 708cm ÷ 6

i) 14cm 1mm ÷ 3

4. If every brick in the wall is 25cm 7mm high and the wall is 8 bricks high, what is the exact height of the wall?

5. Barry walked to school 3 days this week. If he walked a total distance of 2km 58m over the 3 days, how far is the school from his house?

6. If a row of terraced houses stretches 68.95m and there are 5 houses in the row, how wide is each house?

Estimate Length and Choose Appropriate Units of Measurement

List all the instruments that you can think of that are used to measure lengths or distances. Compare your list with the people around you. If there are any that you have not heard of before, find out what they are used to measure.

Can you estimate how wide this maths book is? What unit of measurement did you use to make your guess? I bet it wasn't kilometres.

7. Estimate the following using the most appropriate units of measurement.

a) The width of your copy

b) The length of the blackboard/whiteboard

c) The width of a window in the classroom

d) The thickness of your copy

e) The height of your teacher

8. Fill in this table. Decide first what units of measurement are most appropriate. Make your estimate. Measure to see how close you were. Calculate the difference between your estimate and the actual measurement. State what instrument you used to measure.

Object	Unit	Estimate	Measurement	Difference	Instrument
Height of the door					
Width of the class					
Thickness of a rubber					
Length of the yard					
Length of your pencil					

Perimeter

Perimeter is a measure of the distance you would travel if you walked around the outside of a shape.

1. If a small snail slipped and slithered along the perimeter of this shape, how far would it have travelled?

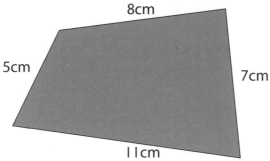

8cm

5cm

7cm

11cm

2. Run your finger along the outside of your maths book. Now work out what distance your finger has travelled. Compare your answer with those of the people near you.

3. Work out the perimeters of these shapes.

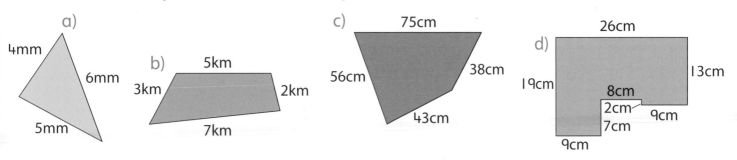

a)
4mm
6mm
5mm

b)
5km
3km
2km
7km

c)
75cm
56cm
38cm
43cm

d)
26cm
19cm
13cm
8cm
2cm
9cm
7cm
9cm

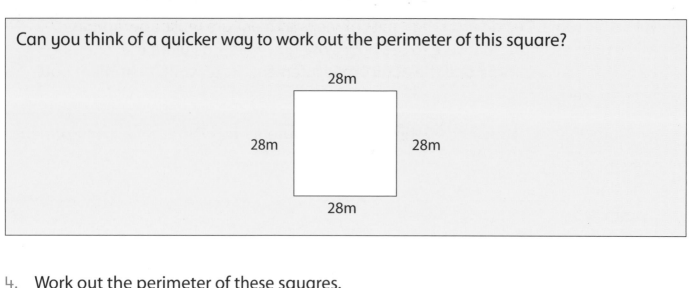

Can you think of a quicker way to work out the perimeter of this square?

28m

28m   28m

28m

4. Work out the perimeter of these squares.
    a) length 37mm
    b) length 49m
    c) length 134cm
    d) length 365km
    e) length 3m 4cm
    f) length 5km 38m

5. Calculate the perimeters of these equilateral triangles. Remember: an equilateral triangle has 3 equal sides.
    a) length 3.7cm
    b) length 4.93m
    c) length 1.685km
    d) length 549mm
    e) length $3\frac{1}{4}$m
    f) length 3km 182m

The 4 sides of a rectangle are not all the same lengths, but there is still a quick way of calculating its perimeter. Can you figure it out?

37cm

19cm   19cm

37cm

6. Now work out the perimeters of these rectangles.
    a) length 46cm
        width 28cm
    b) length 83mm
        width 45mm
    c) length 116m
        width 74m
    d) length 9.3cm
        width 4.7cm
    e) length 1.08m
        width 0.79m
    f) length 3.512km
        width 1.466km

7. Farmer Joan's field is 83m long and 54m wide. Farmer Roy's field is 68m long and 62m wide. Which field has the longer perimeter?

8. The perimeter of a square in a copy is 36mm. What is the length of a side of that square?

9. A football pitch has a perimeter of 340m. If the pitch is 60m wide, how long is it?

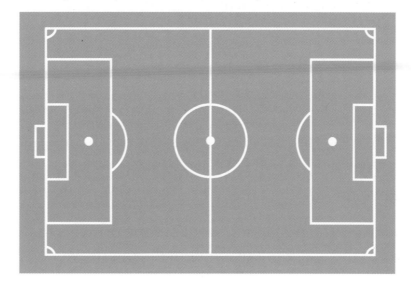

Homework

1. Fill in the blanks.

a) 1m 87cm = _____cm

b) 209cm = ___m _____cm

c) 3m 45cm = _____m

d) 5m 3cm = _____m

e) 2096m = ___km _____m

f) 8km 752m = _____m

g) 1.28km = _____m

h) 984m = _____km

2. Now try these. You can choose to solve them whichever way you prefer, but it is very important that you record the unit of measurement in your answer.

a) 2m 4cm + 116cm + 3.57m

b) 68cm + 5m 29cm + 7.36m

c) $2\frac{2}{5}$m + 108cm + 6.48m

d) 8m 48cm + 5.75m

e) $6\frac{3}{4}$m + 326cm + 6.57m

f) 1.97m + 4m 78cm + 63cm

3. Now do the same thing with subtraction.

a) 5m 19cm – 265cm

b) 7.12m – 4m 58cm

c) 726cm – 3.8m

d) 9m 14cm – 7.86m

e) 3m 34cm – 195cm

f) $6\frac{3}{10}$m – 4m 46cm

4. Now try these.

a) 7km 47m + 694m + 3.28km

b) $1\frac{85}{1000}$km + 4km 573m + 6037m

c) 8.19km + $5\frac{3}{5}$km + 1km 469m

d) 3km 2m + 3.82km + 290m

e) 8km 192m – 5.687km

f) 6285m – 4km 78m

g) 9.08km – 583m

h) $7\frac{3}{4}$km – 5km 804m

5. Fill in the blanks.

    a) 19mm = ___cm ___mm   b) 3cm 9mm = ___cm   c) 5.4cm = ___mm

    d) 6cm 2mm = ___mm   e) 117mm = ___cm ___mm   f) ___cm = 15cm 7mm

6. Now try these.

    a) 4cm 6mm + 32mm + 1.9cm   b) $84mm + 4\frac{2}{5}cm + 7cm\ 5mm$

    c) $118mm + 6.7cm + 14\frac{7}{10}cm$ d) $2\frac{3}{5}cm + 5cm\ 3mm + 7.8cm$

    e) 8cm 1mm – 49mm   f) 123mm – 9.6cm

    g) 11.4cm – 7cm 7mm   h) 13cm 5mm – 126mm

7. Choose whichever way you prefer and work out the answers to these.
   Remember to record the unit of measurement in your answer.

    a) 7m 19cm × 7   b) 186cm × 9   c) 4.84m × 6

    d) 5km 78m × 8   e) 8.205km × 11   f) 5492m × 5

8. Now try these.

    a) 195mm ÷ 5   b) 1km 876m ÷ 7   c) 41.67m ÷ 9

    d) 25m 36cm ÷ 8   e) 47.4cm ÷ 6   f) 2016m ÷ 12

9. Now work out the perimeters of these rectangles.

    a) length 29cm   b) length 69mm   c) length 126m
       width 35cm   width 38mm   width 57m

    d) length 8.4cm   e) length 2.17m   f) length 4.476km
       width 2.5cm   width 0.68m   width 2.387km

Recap

- I can add and subtract m and cm.   ○ ○ ○

- I can add and subtract km and m.   ○ ○ ○

- I can write cm as mm and vice versa.   ○ ○ ○

- I can multiply and divide lengths.   ○ ○ ○

- I can estimate length and choose appropriate units
  of measurement.   ○ ○ ○

- I know what perimeter is.   ○ ○ ○

- I can calculate perimeter.   ○ ○ ○

22. 3-D Shapes

Talk About

Puzzler

If 2-D shapes have 2 dimensions (length and width) and 3-D shapes have 3 dimensions, what is the third dimension? Discuss what you would call this third dimension with the people near you.

If you go into a sweet shop where they keep the sweets in jars on shelves behind the counter, you will notice that some of the sweets are regular 3-D shapes. Can you think of a type of sweet in each of these 3-D shapes?

3-D Shape	Type of Sweet
Sphere	
Cube	
Cuboid	
Cylinder	

Cubes

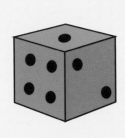  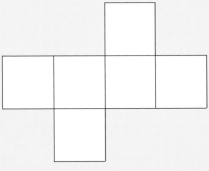

Copy this set of squares exactly onto a piece of paper. Then cut it out, fold it where the squares meet and stick it together to make a die of your own. Draw the correct number of dots on each of the faces. Use a real die to help you.

Strand: Shape and Space
Curriculum Objectives:
Make, identify and examine 3-D shapes and explore relationships, including tetrahedron (faces, edges and vertices); draw the nets of simple 3-D shapes and construct the shapes.

157

Did you know that the word 'dice' is actually the plural of the word 'die'? So if you are playing a game with only 1, you should say 'roll the die' instead of 'roll the dice.'

1. What shape is the die?

2. How many faces does the die have? (Hint: there are dots that represent numbers on each of the faces, which might give you a clue.)

3. Can you suggest what practical difficulties there might be if we used the following 3-D shapes as dice?
   a) sphere   b) cuboid

4. a) Why do most dice have rounded corners?

   b) Count the number of corners (vertices) on a cube (die).

5. What do you notice about the opposite faces of the die?
   (Hint: try combining the numbers.)

6. Now that we know what the faces and corners (vertices) of a cube are, what do you think the edges are? How many of them are there?

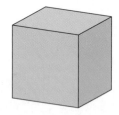 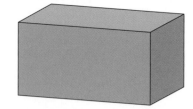

7. A cuboid has the same number of faces, edges and vertices as a cube, so what is the difference between a cube and a cuboid?

8. Examine the following 3-D shapes and then fill in the table.

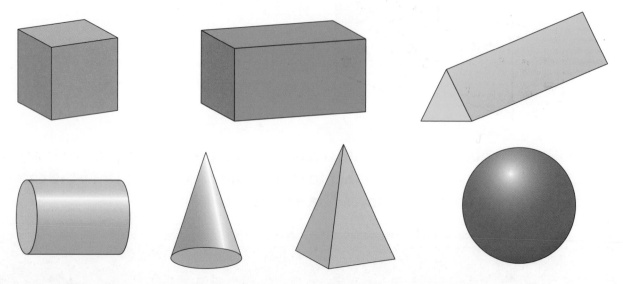

	Cube	Cuboid	Cylinder	Pyramid	Sphere	Cone	Triangular Prism
Number of faces							
Number of edges							
Number of corners							
All the faces are flat							
There are no flat faces							

List all the 3-D shapes that only have flat faces. We call these shapes **polyhedrons**. Can you think of any other polyhedrons?

9. a) What different 2-D shapes make up a pyramid?

b) What do a cylinder and a sphere have in common?

c) How many different rectangles make up the sides of a cuboid?

10. What 3-D shapes are these objects usually? Fill in the table.

Object	Shape
Cupboard	
Tin of beans	
Book	
Globe	
Funnel	
Carton of milk	
Car wheel	
Ice cream cone	

11. Some objects are made up of a combination of 3-D shapes. Examine this picture of a round tower and list the shapes.

12. List 5 objects that are made up of more than 1 3-D shape.

13. What different 3-D shapes make up the following objects?

   a)

   b)

14. Carefully cut open a cereal box along its edges. When you open it up, it should look like one of the following.

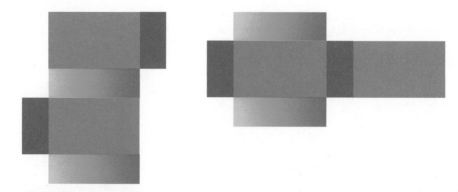

   Now put the box back together again. Label each flap with a letter and then write out a series of instructions for assembly, referring to the lettered flaps.

A 3-D shape that has been opened up like so is called a **net**.

15. Look at these possible nets for a cube. Which ones can be assembled into cubes and which ones cannot?

a)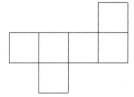

b)

c)

d)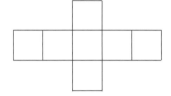

e)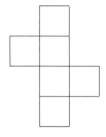

16. Study these nets and suggest what shapes they are.

a)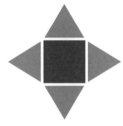

b)

A 3-D shape where every face is flat and of the same size and shape is called a **regular polyhedron**. Can you think of any 3-D shape that could be called a regular polyhedron?

A shape made up completely of equilateral triangles is called a **tetrahedron**. Copy this net of a tetrahedron onto a piece of paper. Then cut it out and assemble it.

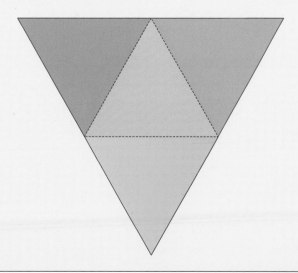

17. How many a) faces b) edges and c) vertices does a tetrahedron have?
Is a tetrahedron a regular polyhedron? Explain your answer.

18. a) Look at this net. Apart from looking like a robot's head, what 3-D shape do you think it makes?

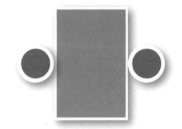

b) Copy it onto a piece of paper, cut it out and assemble it.

c) Is it a polyhedron? Explain your answer.

19. True or false?

a) A cube has 8 edges.

b) A cuboid is a regular polyhedron.

c) A pyramid has 5 faces.

d) A triangular prism is a regular polyhedron.

e) A tetrahedron has 6 edges.

f) An octagonal prism has 10 faces.

g) A sphere is not a polyhedron.

h) A cylinder is a prism.

20. With the 3-D shapes that you have assembled, construct an unusual building or cityscape. Work with the people who are near you.

Homework

1. See if you can find examples of the following 3-D shapes in your house.

a) cube   b) sphere   c) cuboid

d) cylinder   e) cone   f) pyramid

2. Name the following 3-D shapes from their nets.

a) 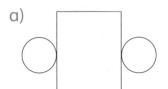   b) 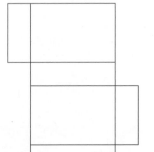   c) 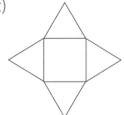   d)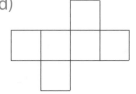

3. Choose 1 of the nets above and construct the 3-D shape.

4. Are the following 3-D shapes regular polyhedrons?

Shape	Yes	No
Cuboid		
Pyramid		
Cube		
Cylinder		
Tetrahedron		
Triangular prism		

Recap

- I can identify 3-D shapes. ○ ○ ○

- I can recognise and assemble 3-D shapes from their nets. ○ ○ ○

- I can identify characteristics of particular 3-D shapes. ○ ○ ○

23. Percentages

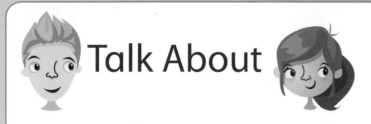

Talk About

The word 'percent' means 'for each hundred.'

The word 'cent' is found in a lot of different words: centimetre, centipede, century and 1 cent. What do you think each one of these words means?

Write Fractions and Decimals as Percentages

Like fractions and decimals, we use percent to describe a proportion or a quantity.

There were 100 questions in the test and Jessica got 78 right.

We can express this as $\frac{78}{100}$, 0.78 or 78%. Each means 78 out of 100.

$$\frac{78}{100} = 0.78 = 78\%$$

We use the percent symbol (%) to express percent.

1. Write these results as a decimal and percentage.

   a) $\frac{55}{100} = 0.$ ___ = ___%

   b) $\frac{89}{100} = 0.$ ___ = ___%

2. Express these fractions as percentages.

   a) $\frac{22}{100}$ 　 b) $\frac{7}{100}$ 　 c) $\frac{99}{100}$ 　 d) $\frac{51}{100}$ 　 e) $\frac{30}{100}$ 　 f) $\frac{1}{100}$

   g) $\frac{84}{100}$ 　 h) $\frac{62}{100}$ 　 i) $\frac{9}{100}$ 　 j) $\frac{76}{100}$ 　 k) $\frac{100}{100}$ 　 l) $\frac{13}{100}$

Strand: Number
Curriculum Objectives:
Develop an understanding of simple percentages and relate them to fractions and decimals;
solve problems involving operations with whole numbers, fractions, decimals and simple percentages.

3. What percentage of each of these is red; blue; white?

a)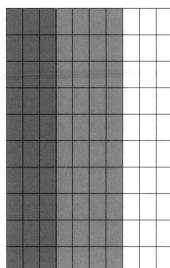
b)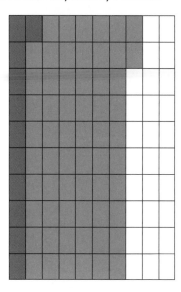
c)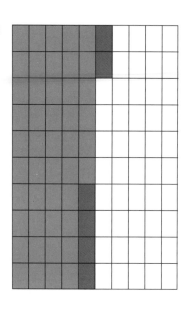

Write Percentages as Fractions and Decimals

4. Express these percentages as fractions.

   a) $35\% = \frac{}{100}$
   b) 2%
   c) 77%
   d) 23%

   e) 90%
   f) 16%
   g) 81%
   h) 49%

   i) 8%
   j) 10%
   k) 66%
   l) 50%

5. Draw 100-squares and shade in the following.

   a) 27%
   b) 52%
   c) 94%

   d) 14%
   e) 38%
   f) 71%

Find a Percentage of a Number

6. I had 100 sweets and I shared out 68 among my friends.

   a) What percentage of the sweets did I share?

   b) What percentage of the sweets did I have left?

7. There are 100 pages in the book I started reading and I read $\frac{23}{100}$ of it last night.

   a) What percentage did I read?

   b) What percentage do I have left to read?

Calculate Percentages

Fractions are not always written as hundredths, so before we change them to percentages, we need to write them as equivalent fractions with a denominator of 100:

$$\frac{1}{10} = \frac{1}{10} \times \frac{10}{10} = \frac{10}{100} = 10\%$$

$$\frac{2}{5} = \frac{2}{5} \times \frac{20}{20} = \frac{40}{100} = \_\_\_\%$$

Have a go!

1. Convert the fractions to hundredths and then percentages.

   a) $\frac{1}{5} = \frac{}{100} = $ ___%

   b) $\frac{3}{10}$

   c) $\frac{3}{4}$

   d) $\frac{7}{10}$

   e) $\frac{1}{2}$

   f) $\frac{9}{10}$

   g) $\frac{1}{4}$

   h) $\frac{4}{5}$

   i) $\frac{3}{5}$

2. Write the following percentages as a fraction with a denominator of 100 and then reduce them to their lowest terms.

   a) $70\% = \frac{}{100} = \frac{}{10}$

   b) 25%

   c) 50%

   d) 20%

   e) 95%

   f) 62%

   g) 80%

   h) 2%

   i) 75%

Tom had €1.00 and bought some sweets for €0.36.
What percentage of the money did he spend?
What percentage did he have left?

$$0.36 = \frac{36}{100} = 36\% \text{ money spent}$$
$$1.00 - 0.36 = 0.64 \text{ money left}$$
$$0.64 = \frac{64}{100} = 64\%$$

---

3. Convert these decimals to fractions and then percentages.

   a) $0.68 = \frac{}{100} = $ ___%

   b) 0.33

   c) 0.05

   d) 0.99

   e) 0.18

   f) 0.42

   g) 0.27

   h) 0.06

   i) 0.71

4. Now try these. Remember to convert them to fractions with a denominator of 100 first.

   a) $0.7 = \frac{}{10} = \frac{}{100} = $ ___%

   b) 0.1

   c) 0.3

   d) 0.5

   e) 0.2

   f) 0.8

   g) 0.9

   h) 0.4

   i) 0.6

5. Complete this table.

Decimal	Fraction	Percentage
0.92		
		10%
	$\frac{3}{10}$	
0.06		
		75%
	$\frac{17}{100}$	
0.5		
		100%
	$\frac{2}{5}$	
0.48		

6. Pick 6 television programmes and ask 20 people in your class to pick their favourite. Fill in the information on a chart like this:

TV Programme	Fraction	Decimal	%
	$\overline{20}$		
	$\overline{20}$		
	$\overline{20}$		

7. a) If Jill used 45% of a bag of sugar to bake a cake, what percentage of the bag was left?

   b) Grace got 98% on a spelling test. What percentage of the spellings did she get wrong?

   c) Marcus used 30% of his petrol driving to Kerry. What percentage did he have left to get him home again?

Sometimes when changing a fraction or a decimal to a percentage, we don't get a whole number as the percentage.

$$\frac{1}{8} = \frac{12\frac{1}{2}}{100} = 0.125 = 12\frac{1}{2}\%$$ $$\frac{1}{3} = \frac{33\frac{1}{3}}{100} = 0.333 = 33\frac{1}{3}\%$$

8. Can you change the following fractions to decimals and then percentages?

   a) $\frac{3}{8}$ b) $\frac{2}{3}$ c) $\frac{5}{8}$ d) $\frac{7}{8}$

Ross is reading a book that has 60 pages. If he read 50% of the book in 1 week, how many pages did he read?

$50\% = \frac{50}{100} = \frac{1}{2}$

$\frac{1}{2}$ of 60 = 60 ÷ 2 = 30

So Ross read 30 pages.

9. Try these.

   a) 50% of 160 pages = $\frac{1}{2}$ of 160 = _____ pages

   b) 50% of 200 pages = _____ pages

   c) 50% of 90 pages = _____ pages

   d) 100% of 70 pages = _____ pages

   e) 25% of 80 pages = $\frac{25}{100} = \frac{1}{4}$ of 80 = _____ pages

   f) 25% of 36 pages = _____ pages

We can now find 50% and 25% of a number by converting them to fractions and then finding that fraction of the number.

25% of 40 = $\frac{1}{4}$ of 40 = 10

10. Can you work out the following percentages of 40 in the same way?

a) 20% of 40 = $\frac{20}{100}$ = $\frac{1}{5}$ of 40 = _____

b) 10% of 40 = $\frac{10}{100}$ = $\frac{1}{10}$ of 40 = _____

11. Fill in the blanks in this table.

	100	200	60	20
100%	100			
50%		100		
25%			15	
20%				
10%				2

Calculate Percentage Increases

 Puzzler

The Delaneys went out to dinner and their bill came to a total of €85. If they wanted to leave a tip of 15%, how much should they leave?

12. These are the results of today's maths quiz. There were 30 questions in the quiz. Work out how many questions each person got correct.

a) Rachel: 50%   b) Tobias: 100%   c) Claire: 60%

 Remember: to find a percentage of a number, change the percentage to a fraction in its lowest terms and find that fraction of the number.

30% of 120 = $\frac{30}{100}$ = $\frac{1}{10}$ of 120

$\frac{1}{10}$ = 120 ÷ 10 = 12

$\frac{3}{10}$ = 12 × 3 = 36

13. Try these in the same way.

a) 60% of 70   b) 10% of 320   c) 5% of 400

d) 30% of 140   e) 45% of 80   f) 90% of 650

g) 7% of 200   h) 56% of 125   i) 75% of 24

j) 80% of 40   k) 3% of 500   l) 22% of 350

14. Laura delivers newspapers to houses in her area at the weekend. She has 90 to deliver and on Saturday she delivered 40% of them. How many papers will she have to deliver on Sunday?

15. Ben had €1.80 and spent 70% of the money on a comic. How much money did he have left?

16. At a soccer match, Aisling scored 60% of the 5 goals. How many goals did she score?

17. Of the 56 apples in a box, $12\frac{1}{2}$% were rotten. How many good apples were there?

18. There are 380 cars in the car park. Work out how many there are of each make.

Toyota	10%
Mazda	5%
Fiat	25%
Nissan	5%
Ford	40%
Peugeot	15%

Estimate

1. A football stadium holds 2500 people. At the match on Saturday it was 63% full. Estimate how many people were at the match.

   63% to the nearest 10 is 60% and 60% $= \frac{3}{5}$

   $\frac{3}{5}$ of 2500 people = _____ people

2. Estimate the following.

   a) 9% of 270
   b) 48% of 1280
   c) 74% of 40
   d) 21% of 520
   e) 17% of 325
   f) 93% of 70

Percentage Recipes

3. Here is a recipe for chocolate chip cookies. The total weight of the ingredients is 400g. Work out how many grams of each dry ingredient are needed.

   20% margarine   25% caster sugar
   45% self-raising flour 10% chocolate chips
   plus 1 large egg $\frac{1}{2}$ tsp vanilla extract

4. To go with the cookies, here is a recipe for orange punch. If the bowl will hold 500ml, how many millilitres of each ingredient are there?

60% orange   30% lemon   10% lime

5. Make up a few recipes of your own and write the ingredients in percentages.

Percentage Power

6. a) Find 25% of 200 on your calculator using only these keys: 200, ×, 25, %.

   b) Find 50% of 80 using only these keys: 80, ×, 50, %.

7. Define a rule for finding percentages with a calculator.

8. Now try these with your calculator.

a) 32% of 2600	b) 98% of 1350	c) 2% of 350
d) 16% of 1900	e) 85% of 80	f) 41% of 950
g) 18% of 750	h) 53% of 3400	i) 8% of 325
j) 69% of 40	k) 27% of 960	l) 78% of 1450

Calculating Percentage Discounts

1. Newtown Clothes Store is having a sale. Calculate the sale price of each of the items.

$$\text{Shirt: } 100\% = €25$$
$$20\% = \frac{20}{100} = \frac{1}{5}$$
$$\frac{1}{5} \text{ of } €25 = €5$$
$$€25 - €5 = \underline{\hspace{1cm}}$$

full price − discount = sale price

a) 20% off
   Was €25
   Now _____

b) 15% off
   Was €60
   Now _____

c) 30% off
   Was €65
   Now _____

d) $33\frac{1}{3}$% off
Was €90

Now _____

e) 10% off
Was €75.50

Now _____

2. Calculate the sale price of each item.

Fruit and Veg
25% off all stock
Everything must go!

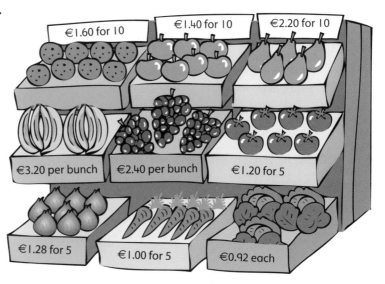

3. During a sale, a television set priced at €472 was reduced by $12\frac{1}{2}$%. What was the sale price?

4. Decrease the following prices by 20%.
   a) €420.00
   b) €25.50
   c) €129.00
   d) €30.60
   e) €2450.00
   f) €99.90
   g) €785.20
   h) €575.10
   i) €8.80

5. A car dealership decided to increase all its car prices by 10%. Calculate the new car prices.

   a) €12500
   b) €14250
   c) €15000
   d) €25100
   e) €29900

The first one has been done for you on the next page.

$$100\% = €12500$$

$$10\% = \frac{10}{100} = \frac{1}{10}$$

$$\frac{1}{10} \text{ of } €12500 = €1250$$

$$€12500 + €1250 = €13750$$

full price + increase = new price

6. An online book store charges a 5% delivery charge on all its orders. Find the price of buying each of the following books online, including the delivery charge.
   a) *Milly the Musical Mule* – €6.80
   b) *Cyril the Squirrel* – €9.40
   c) *Nigel the Gnome* – €12.20
   d) *Not Now, Nick!* – €4.60
   e) *Killer Cupcakes* – €5.20
   f) *The Revenge of Rick the Raisin* – €7.40

7. Increase the following prices by 50%.
   a) €290.00
   b) €10.40
   c) €2365.00
   d) €34.50
   e) €928.00
   f) €78.16
   g) €5690.10
   h) €120.80
   i) €6.40

8. Increase these lengths by 75%.
   a) 100m
   b) 16cm
   c) 244m
   d) 4cm
   e) 32.8cm
   f) 104.4m
   g) 12.8m
   h) 760m
   i) 40cm

9. During a promotion, a manufacturer decided to add 20% extra free to the following items. Calculate the total amount of each product.

   a) apple juice 500ml
   b) pasta 400g
   c) curry sauce 240g
   d) blackcurrant juice 120ml
   e) biscuits 360g

10. Caroline has €4.50. Sarah has 20% more money than Caroline. How much money does Sarah have?

11. Brendan is buying a new computer costing €1360. For an extra $12\frac{1}{2}$% he can also have a scanner. How much is the total package?

12. After Christmas, a shop decided to increase all its prices. Calculate the new price for each item.

Item	Price	% Increase	New Price
Stereo	€690	10%	
Television	€480	25%	
DVD	€240	$33\frac{1}{3}$%	
MP3 player	€35.80	5%	
Camcorder	€820	45%	
Digital camera	€950	30%	

Homework

1. Express these fractions as percentages.

   a) $\frac{8}{100}$ b) $\frac{17}{100}$ c) $\frac{76}{100}$ d) $\frac{39}{100}$ e) $\frac{4}{100}$

   f) $\frac{53}{100}$ g) $\frac{92}{100}$ h) $\frac{68}{100}$ i) $\frac{3}{100}$

2. Express these percentages as fractions.

   a) $71\% = \frac{}{100}$ b) 29% c) 7% d) 14% e) 84%

   f) 36% g) 93% h) 55% i) 48%

3. Convert these decimals to fractions and then percentages.

   a) $0.19 = \frac{}{100} = $ _____% b) 0.41 c) 0.35

   d) 0.25 e) 0.89 f) 0.02

   g) 0.76 h) 0.66 i) 0.97

4. Find:

   a) 50% of €94 b) 25% of €156 c) 10% of €8.40

   d) 20% of €275 e) 40% of €7.90 f) 75% of €968

5. Now try these.

   a) 70% of 450 b) 30% of 260 c) 90% of 430

   d) $12\frac{1}{2}$% of 152 e) $33\frac{1}{3}$% of 207 f) 5% of 780

6. Now try these using your calculator.
    a) 39% of 1800
    b) 27% of 2050
    c) 8% of 1075
    d) 74% of 8300
    e) 64% of 2950
    f) 55% of 4640

7. Complete this table to show the sale prices.

Item	Old Price	% Discount	Sale Price
Shoes	€95	20%	
MP3 player	€70	40%	
Laptop	€490	10%	
Jeans	€48	$33\frac{1}{3}$%	
Tennis racket	€85	60%	
Bike	€192	$12\frac{1}{2}$%	

8. Complete this table to show the increased prices.

Item	Old Price	% Increase	New Price
Book	€9.40	5%	
Scooter	€130	30%	
TV	€328	25%	
Coat	€120	15%	
Printer	€64	75%	
Games console	€176	$12\frac{1}{2}$%	

Recap

- I can write fractions and decimals as percentages. ○ ○ ○

- I can write percentages as fractions and decimals. ○ ○ ○

- I can find a percentage of a number. ○ ○ ○

- I can calculate percentages. ○ ○ ○

- I can calculate percentage increases. ○ ○ ○

- I can calculate percentage discounts. ○ ○ ○

25. Directed Numbers

 Talk About

Thermometers

1. Here is a Celsius thermometer. We use it to measure temperature.

   a) What temperature does it read?

   b) Do you think this temperature is hot or cold?

   c) What temperature do you think it is outside today?

   d) Fill in the blanks in this sentence: The freezing point of water is at _____°C and the _____ point of water is at 100°C.

   e) Sort the following list into temperatures above freezing point and temperatures below freezing point.

   + 5°C   −3°C   −6°C   +10°C   +8°C   −2°C   +7°C

   f) What average temperature would you expect to find on a summer day in Ireland?

   g) What average temperature would you expect to find in winter in Ireland?

2. Fill in the missing numbers on this section of a thermometer.

3. Which is the warmer temperature?

   a) 2°C or 9°C   b) 10°C or 8°C   c) 1°C or 2°C

   d) 12°C or 6°C   e) 7°C or 3°C   f) 5°C or 11°C

   g) −3°C or 0°C   h) −2°C or 1°C

4. Which is the colder temperature?

   a) 7°C or 2°C   b) 1°C or 9°C   c) 3°C or 4°C

   d) 0°C or 10°C   e) 1°C or −3°C   f) −5°C or −2°C

   g) −4°C or −7°C   h) −8°C or −1°C

Strand: Algebra
Curriculum Objectives:
Identify positive and negative numbers in context.

5. Draw thermometers to show the following scales.

   a) −4°C to 6°C   b) − 8°C to 5°C   c) −10°C to 2°C   d) − 7°C to 7°C

6. A meteorologist recorded temperatures in 8 cities around the world in January.
   List these temperatures in order from coldest to the hottest.

| Chicago | −2°C | Athens | 15°C | Dublin | 6°C | Helsinki | −5°C |
| Cairo | 13°C | Sydney | 22°C | Moscow | −8°C | Rio de Janeiro | 25°C |

7. What was the difference, in degrees, between the hottest and the coldest temperature?

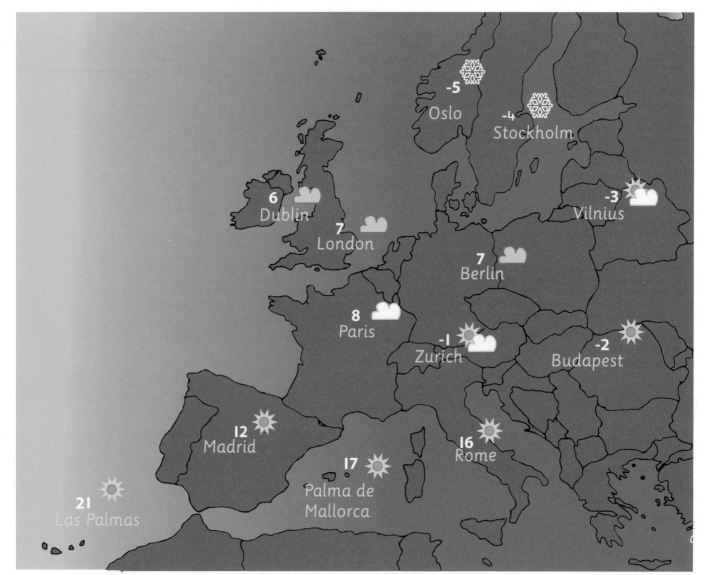

8. From the map, determine the following.

   a) Which city has the lowest temperature today?

   b) Name the city with the highest temperature.

   c) Find the difference in temperature between these 2 cities.

   d) List 4 cities with temperatures below freezing point.

   e) List 4 cities with temperatures above freezing point.

   f) Pick 5 cities and their respective temperatures and put them in order, starting
       with the coldest.

9.

Find a lift in a supermarket, car park or hotel and investigate what level is below ground level.

Thermometers and lifts give examples of **directed numbers**: the group of numbers that includes both positive and negative numbers, or numbers above and below zero.

Whole numbers greater than zero are called **positive numbers**.

When writing a positive number, for example a positive five, we write either 5 or +5. Whole numbers less than zero are called **negative numbers**. When writing a negative number, for example a negative five, we write −5.

10. Write down these numbers using the appropriate symbols: + or −.

a) positive 9 = +___   b) positive 13   c) negative 4   d) positive 20

e) negative 10   f) negative 8   g) positive 3   h) negative 15

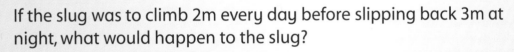

Puzzler

A slug is 25m down a 50m-deep vertical tunnel. Every day it crawls up 3m before slipping back 2m every night. How many days will it take to get to the top of the shaft?

If the slug was to climb 2m every day before slipping back 3m at night, what would happen to the slug?

11. Directed numbers appear in a variety of situations. Write these as directed numbers.

a) Temperature of 6 degrees Celsius below zero

b) The number in a lift for the second floor of a hotel

c) A submarine travelling 100 metres below sea level

d) Temperature of 18 degrees Celsius above zero

e) Climbing a mountain 200 metres above sea level

f) A loss of €25

g) A gain of 5 points

Height above or below **sea level** is measured in metres. Sea level is exactly 0.
Altitude is the name given for height above sea level.

Can you think of anything that would be measured in metres above or below sea level? Discuss with the person beside you.

12. Fill in this table.

	Positive/Negative Number
A plane flying at 9000m above sea level	+_____m
A diver diving 10m below sea level	_____m
A submarine _____	−350m
A mountain peak at 1260m above sea level	_____m
A glider gliding at an altitude of 550m	_____m
A shipwreck 12m below sea level	_____m
Standing on a _____	+80m
A hot air balloon travelling at an altitude of 300m	_____m

Money

1. Amanda was organising to buy Christmas presents for her parents and younger brother. She has saved €10 and wants to buy the following.

a) Imagining that Amanda bought these 3 presents, what would the balance of her money be? –€_____

Amanda would owe €_____, or be in **debit** to this amount.

b) If Amanda bought only the train and the book, what would the balance be?
€_____

Amanda would have €_____ left, or be in **credit** to this amount.

c) Find out what the terms debit, credit and overdraft mean.

2. Solve this using directed numbers. Jenny earns €10, spends €6, earns €2 and spends €8. How many euros does she have or owe?

Golf uses directed numbers in its scoring. This table shows the scores of the first round of the Golf Open Championships.

Name	Score
Appledy	76
Ellis	66
Wood	70
Harring	72
Evan	75
O'Malley	73
McCarron	69
Dorman	68

The number of golf strokes (or par) the golfers should have taken for this course was 71. So if a golfer scored 74, they would have a score of +3, or 3 over par.

If a golfer scored 67, they would have a score of –4, or 4 under par.

The winner is the golfer who is the most under par or takes the least amount of strokes to complete the course.

3. Using the information given in the table, work out how much over or under par each of the players was.

4. Answer these questions from the final scores you have found.
   a) How many strokes separate Dorman from O'Malley? –3 to +2 = _____
   b) How many fewer strokes did it take Ellis to complete the course than Evan?
   c) How many strokes separate Wood from McCarron?
   d) What is the difference in score between Harring and Appledy?
   e) Who is in the lead in this round?

5. 5th class have drawn up a league table to show the results of their Unihoc League.

Teams	Played	Won	Lost	Draw	Goals For	Goals Against	Points	Goal Difference
Lions	3	2	0	1	12	8	5	+4
Panthers	3	1	0	2	9	6	4	+?
Tigers	3	0	1	2	6	9	2	– ?
Gazelles	3	0	2	1	6	10	1	–?

Examine the table and then answer the questions that follow.

a) Fill in the missing information in the table.

goals scored for the team – goals scored against the team = goal difference

For example: 12 – 8 = +4

b) Which teams did not win any matches?

c) Name the team that scored the most goals.

d) In the Goal Difference column, how many goals separate the Lions from the Panthers?

e) How many goals separate the Tigers from the Gazelles?

f) How many goals separate the Lions from the Gazelles?

g) Which team won the Unihoc League?

h) Draw a similar table to record the results of 1 of your own leagues in school.

Homework

1. Use positive or negative numbers to represent the following.
   a) 26 degrees above zero
   b) Diving at 12m below sea level
   c) Account overdrawn by €15
   d) 1 floor below ground level on a lift
   e) 1000m above sea level

2. In Reykjavik, the morning temperature was −12°C. By midday the temperature had risen by 4°C. What was the temperature at midday?

3. Mr Rich had €35 in the bank. He wrote a cheque for €40 to pay a bill. What is his bank balance now?

4. If a golfer had a score of 5 under par upon completion of a course in which the par was 73, how many strokes did it take her to complete the course?

5. Find the result of a recent golf tournament, either in a newspaper, on television or online, and work out how much over or under par each of the players was.

6. Make up 5 questions based on the table of results you have found.

Recap

- I can identify directed numbers on a number line. ○ ○ ○

- I can order directed numbers. ○ ○ ○

- I can add directed numbers. ○ ○ ○

- I can add directed numbers in different contexts. ○ ○ ○

26. Weight

Talk About

Instruments to Use When Weighing

1. Have a look at the items in your school bag and on your table and decide how heavy each item would be. Estimate which of these items would be closest to 10g, 100g, 500g or 1kg.

    a) Make a list of these items with the corresponding estimate beside each.

    b) Which item do you think is the heaviest and which is the lightest?

    c) How would you weigh each item to check your estimate?

2. a) Can you identify the following instruments used for weighing objects?

    b) Give an example of where you might find each instrument.

    c) Name 2 items you would weigh using each of the above instruments.

    Remember: 1000 grams (g) = 1 kilogram (kg)

    1 gram = 0.001 kilogram = $\frac{1}{1000}$kg

3. Estimate which item is heavier.

    a) A basketball or a balloon

    b) A ceramic cup or a tin cup

    c) A wooden box or an iron box of the same size

    d) A kilogram of coal or a kilogram of feathers

    e) A bag of air or a bag of water

    f) What instrument would you use to weigh each of these items?

Strand: Measures
Curriculum Objectives:
Select and use appropriate instruments of measurement;
estimate and measure weight using appropriate metric units.

Units of Measurement

1. Find out which of the following items is the lightest. First estimate the weight of each, then select the appropriate unit and weigh them using the appropriate instrument.

   a) compass
   b) lunchbox
   c) schoolbag
   d) calculator
   e) piece of fruit
   f) bottle of paint
   g) maths book
   h) yourself

2. Put these items in order, starting with the heaviest item.

   600g   400g   2.5kg   300g   1kg

3. Can you write these as grams?

   a) 2 kilograms
   b) $\frac{1}{2}$ kilogram
   c) $\frac{1}{4}$ kilogram
   d) $\frac{3}{4}$ kilogram
   e) $\frac{235}{1000}$ kilograms
   f) $3\frac{1}{2}$ kilograms

4. Choose the correct unit.

   a) Does a bag of flour weigh 1 gram or 1 kilogram?
   b) Does a tin of beans weigh 400 grams or 400 kilograms?
   c) Does a feather weigh 1 gram or 1 kilogram?
   d) Does a school chair weigh 5 grams or 5 kilograms?
   e) Does a bag of coal weigh 25 grams or 25 kilograms?
   f) Does a bicycle weigh 10 grams or 10 kilograms?
   g) Does a mobile phone weigh 150 grams or 150 kilograms?

5. Find 6 books in your classroom of different weights.

   a) Estimate how heavy each one is. Put them in order of estimated weight from the heaviest to the lightest.

   b) Weigh them and record your answers in as many forms as possible. For example: $2\frac{1}{2}$kg or 2500g or 2.5kg or 2kg 500g.

6. What do these weigh?

   a)   b)   c)   d)

   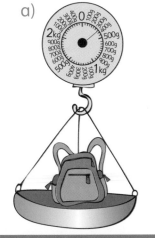         

7. Complete the table. Remember: 1000g = 1kg.

g	kg g	kg
1780g		
	8kg 706g	
		4.952kg
2043g		
	7kg 9g	
		5.38kg
	9kg 25g	
		3.7kg
1007g		

8. Match the object to the correct weight.
   a) A small car   1kg
   b) Fridge   3kg
   c) Portable television   920kg
   d) Laptop computer   7kg
   e) Kettle   25kg

Adding Weights

1. If Mary's schoolbag weighs 4685g, Donal's weighs 3kg 150g and Danielle's weighs 2.4kg, what is the total weight of the schoolbags?

   When adding weights, each weight must be written using the same units. Here are the 3 possibilities:

   a)
   ```
           g
       4685
       3150
   +   2400
   _____
   ```

   b)
   ```
     kg     g
      4    685
      3    150
   +  2    400
   _____
   ```

   c)
   ```
          kg
       4.685
       3.150
   +   2.400
   _____
   ```

   Check to see that the answers are the same.

2. Now try these. Remember to change them to the same units before you start.
   a) 2346g + 1kg 240g + 1.4kg   b) 2.14kg + 1560g + 3kg 460g
   c) 5.34kg + 3kg 20g + 1328g   d) 7.8kg + 2035g + 3kg 100g
   e) 654g + 5kg 302g + 6.9kg   f) 3kg 45g + 8.2kg + 25g

3. Here is a recipe for a chocolate cheesecake.

Chocolate Cheesecake	
275g plain chocolate	4 eggs
1.1kg cream cheese	0.3kg chocolate biscuits
200g sugar	75g melted butter
10g cocoa powder	

a) Write all of the ingredients in grams.
b) Find the combined weight of the cream cheese and the chocolate biscuits.
c) How many more grams of chocolate than sugar are needed?
d) How many more grams of sugar than butter are needed?
e) Find the total weight of all the ingredients needed. (Hint: you don't need to find how heavy the eggs are!)
f) If making this cake, what would you use to get accurate measurements of each ingredient?

Subtracting Weights

4. Now try these subtraction questions. Remember to change measurements to the same unit first.

a) 3950g – 2.5kg
b) 6kg 354g – 3055g
c) 8.9kg – 1490g
d) 7869g – 4kg 155g
e) 19kg 600g – 11.5kg
f) 12.2kg – 6kg 45g

5. 3 parcels weigh 750g, 1.3kg and 2kg 435g. How much less than 5kg is their combined weight?

6. Michael weighed 43kg 32g. Unfortunately he had a particularly bad stomach bug and when he weighed himself again he discovered he was 3.146kg lighter. What weight was Michael after the stomach bug?

7. If a box of washing powder weighed 3.45kg, how much would 4 boxes weigh?

Puzzler

John's weighing scales is not set to 0kg when nobody is standing on it, so when John does stand on it and it records his weight as 49kg, we know that it is not his actual weight. When his sister Joan steps on the weighing scales with John, it records their combined weight as 94kg. When Joan steps on the scales by herself, it records her weight as 47kg. What is John's actual weight?

Multiplying Weights

> We can write this in 3 different ways.
>
> | | g | | kg | g | | kg |
> |---|---|---|---|---|---|---|
> | a) | 3450 | b) | 3 | 450 | c) | 3.45 |
> | × | 4 | × | | 4 | × | 4 |
>
> Do you get the same answer for each?

1. Now have a go at these.
   - a) 4.675kg × 3
   - b) 5kg 349g × 5
   - c) 7.4kg × 6
   - d) 3470g × 9
   - e) 8.25kg × 4
   - f) 9804g × 6
   - g) 14kg 120g × 9
   - h) 11.65kg × 25
   - i) 7350g × 19

2. Find the total weight of 7 boxes of apples if each box weighs 6kg 350g.

3. 34 packets of pasta each weighing 1.2kg are placed in a crate weighing $3\frac{1}{2}$kg. Find the total weight of the crate and pasta.

Dividing Weights

> The total weight of 8 turkeys is 52.8kg. Find the weight of 1 turkey.
>
> 8 | 52.8kg
> _____
>   6.6kg

4. Try these division questions. Remember to give the units for each answer.
   - a) 9.588kg ÷ 4
   - b) 6kg 895g ÷ 5
   - c) 4974g ÷ 6
   - d) 14kg 580g ÷ 9
   - e) 13.68kg ÷ 3
   - f) 11kg 494g ÷ 7
   - g) 50.4kg ÷ 12
   - h) 1kg 632g ÷ 17
   - i) 1856g ÷ 32

5. If a box of cornflakes holds 750g, how many bowls of 30g can you get from 1 box?

6. If a tin of peaches is 450g, how many tins can be filled from a container weighing 22.5kg?

Homework

1. Write these as grams.
   a) 4 kilograms
   b) $1\frac{1}{2}$ kilograms
   c) $3\frac{3}{4}$ kilograms
   d) $\frac{17}{1000}$ kilogram
   e) $\frac{391}{1000}$ kilograms
   f) $8\frac{705}{1000}$ kilograms

2. Write each of these first as kg and g, then as kg.
   a) 3986g
   b) 1070g
   c) 836g
   d) 9281g
   e) 65g
   f) 2540g

3. a) 5.98kg + 7240g + 1kg 287g
   b) 4648g + 9kg 276g + 3.4kg
   c) 6kg 296g + 2.094kg + 7510g
   d) 6.4kg + 7308g + 5kg 67g

4. a) 3kg 567g – 936g
   b) 6.04kg – 3kg 37g
   c) 4927g – 1.85kg
   d) 9kg 69g – 3.197kg

5. a) 3kg 243g × 7
   b) 6295g × 6
   c) 8.208kg × 8
   d) 6120g × 19
   e) 8.43kg × 28
   f) 4kg 87g × 16

6. a) 4374g ÷ 6
   b) 4.83kg ÷ 5
   c) 10kg 976g ÷ 7
   d) 4.68kg ÷ 13
   e) 1360g ÷ 16
   f) 2kg 212g ÷ 28

Recap

- I know what instruments to use when weighing. ○ ○ ○
- I know the most appropriate unit of measurement to use. ○ ○ ○
- I can add weights. ○ ○ ○
- I can subtract weights. ○ ○ ○
- I can multiply weights. ○ ○ ○
- I can divide weights. ○ ○ ○

Talk About

Pictograms

Puzzler

Mrs O'Brien needed to go to the shops to pick up some groceries for dinner, but her twin babies were still having their nap so she decided to ask the Spanish student who was staying with them to go for her. Unfortunately, Carlos could not read English and Mrs O'Brien did not know what the groceries were called in Spanish, so this is the list she gave him.

Could this list cause some confusion? Is there another, quicker way she could have written the list? What do you think they are going to have for dinner?

Strand: Data
Curriculum Objectives:
Collect, organise and represent data using pictograms, single and multiple bar charts and simple pie charts; read and interpret pictograms, single and multiple bar charts and pie charts; compile and use simple data sets; use data sets to solve problems.

1. In a local survey, people were asked what hobby they most liked to do in their spare time. Have a look at the pictogram and answer the questions that follow.

Sport	👟👟👟👟👟👟👟👟👟👟👟👟
Reading	📕📕📕📕📕📕📕📕📕📕📕📕📕
Computers	💻💻💻💻💻💻💻💻💻
Music	🎵🎵🎵🎵🎵🎵🎵🎵🎵🎵
Television	📺📺📺📺
Other	⬛⬛⬛⬛⬛⬛

a) Which was the most popular hobby?

b) How many people were surveyed?

c) Which was the least popular hobby of the people surveyed?

d) How many people liked to participate most in sport?

e) How many more people liked reading than television?

f) Which hobby was 3 times as popular as television?

g) What time of year do you think this survey was carried out? Why do you think so?

h) What hobbies do you think might be included in the 'Other' category?

2. Carry out an investigation to find your classmates' favourite fruit.

In order to tackle this task, first we need to collect data, or the information we need to answer this task. Organise a data sheet similar to this one with appropriate fruit to record your information.

Ask 10 children sitting near you to choose their favourite fruit from the list. Record your data and show your findings on a **pictogram**. 1 piece of fruit equals 1 child. All pictures must be the same size.

Fruit	Number of Children
Apple	
Orange	
Banana	
Pear	
Grapes	
None of these	

3. Collect data from 15 of your classmates about the way they travel to school. Organise your findings on a data sheet and then represent them on a pictogram.

Bar Charts

4. This **bar chart** shows the results of a survey on favourite colours.
   a) How many children were surveyed?
   b) Which was the most popular colour?
   c) Which was the least popular colour?
   d) How many children preferred red to orange?
   e) How many children chose yellow?
   f) What percentage of the group surveyed said that green was their favourite colour?
   g) Which colour would you have chosen?
   h) Carry out a similar investigation in your own class. Record your results on a bar chart.

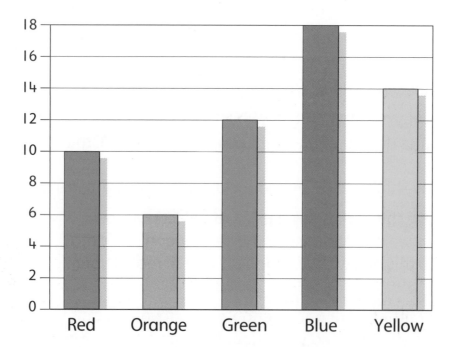

5. Choose 5 popular TV programmes and survey all the children in your class to find their favourite programme from your list. Display your results on a bar chart.

6. Design a table to collect information on the month of each person's birthday in your class. Display your results on a bar chart and answer these questions.
   a) Which month has the greatest number of birthdays?
   b) Name the month with the least number of birthdays.
   c) Are there any months with no birthdays?

Remember to label the axes:

Count

Months

7. Compile a list of what you think are the 6 most popular pop groups. Interview 20 people and display your results on a bar chart. Write 4 sentences to describe your findings. Was your favourite pop group the most popular?

8. Have a look at this table of results for goals scored in a local hockey league. Could you display the results on a bar chart?

Team	Number of Goals Scored
Agile Alligators	16
Vigorous Vixens	12
Lively Leopards	15
Athletic Ants	18
Swift Swans	22
Dynamic Ducks	17

9. Laura's dad is a car salesman and gave the following information about the number of each type of car sold last week. Display the results on a bar chart and make up 5 questions based on the bar chart. (Hint: you need to put some thought into the intervals between numbers. What would be the problem if you went up in 1s?)

Volvo: 18   Peugeot: 28   Fiat: 22
Ford: 34   Toyota: 32   Renault: 40

10. Using a stopwatch, record the amount of time 5 of your classmates take to say the 9 times multiplication tables. Show your results on a bar chart. Who took the least number of seconds?

$9 \times 6 = 54$
$9 \times 7 = 63$
$9 \times 8 = 72$

11. a) Why do you think a bar chart is called a bar chart?
    b) How many different ways can you draw a bar chart? (Hint: think of the way you can draw the axes and the bars.)

Multiple Bar Charts

12. The following table and bar chart show how many pens and pencils were bought each day from the school shop. To compare which were selling better on any given day, we need to put both items on the same bar chart. This is called a **multiple bar chart**.

	Monday	Tuesday	Wednesday	Thursday	Friday
Pen	12	14	17	11	15
Pencil	18	12	14	16	8

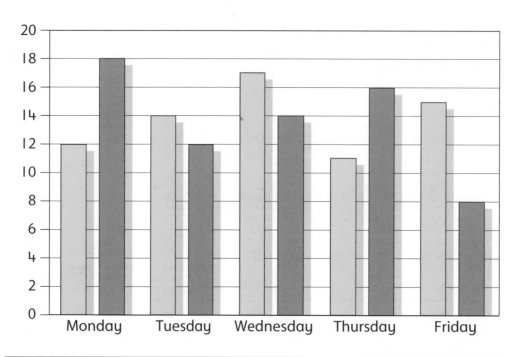

	Monday	Tuesday	Wednesday	Thursday	Friday
Pen	12	14	17	11	15
Pencil	18	12	14	16	8

a) On which days were more pens than pencils sold?

b) On which days were more pencils than pens sold?

c) On what day was there the greatest difference in the amount of pens and pencils sold?

d) How many pens and pencils were sold in total that week?

e) Make up 3 more comparison questions based on the chart.

13. Here is a table following Hilary's test results in each subject for 2 weeks.

a) Plot a multiple bar chart with this information.

	Gaeilge	English	Maths	History	Geography
Week 1	60%	75%	80%	70%	95%
Week 2	70%	55%	85%	80%	90%

b) Write 6 questions based on your graph to puzzle your classmates.

14. Using a thermometer, record the temperature both inside the classroom and outside in the yard at the same time of day for a full week. Construct a table to record your results and then display them on a multiple bar chart.

Pie Charts

A **pie chart** is another way of representing data. It is easy to compare results when they are drawn as sections of a circle.

1. Out of 40 children surveyed, this pie chart represents the number who have a dog, a cat or neither pet at home. Work out the number of children in each section.

a) Cat $= \frac{1}{4}$ of 40 = _____

b) Dog $= \frac{1}{2}$ of 40 = _____

c) Neither $= \frac{1}{4}$ of 40 = _____

In order to represent data on a pie chart, we need to have a look back at fractions and angles.

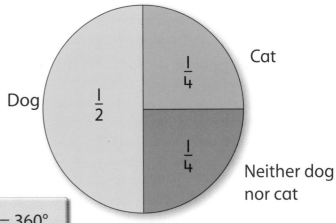

Remember: 1 full rotation = 360°

2. Find:

a) $\frac{1}{2}$ of 360°   b) $\frac{1}{8}$ of 360°   c) $\frac{3}{4}$ of 360°   d) $\frac{1}{10}$ of 360°

3. Match the degrees to the angle: 180°, 45°, 270°, 90°.

a) 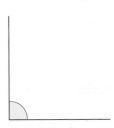   b) 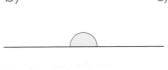   c) 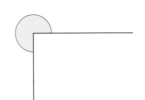   d)

4. What fraction of 360° is each of the following?

    a) 180°   b) 90°   c) 60°   d) 20°

5. Have a look at this pie chart.

    a) What fraction of the circle is represented by each letter? A = _____

    b) If the pie chart represents 80 vegetables on a vegetable stall, work out how many of each type there are if A = potatoes, B = carrots, C = cabbages, D = onions.

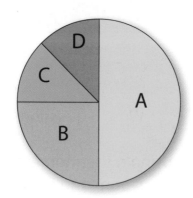

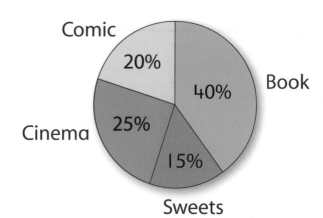

6. This pie chart shows how Oliver spent his €20 birthday money. From the percentages given, can you work out how much money he spent on each item? For example:

    cinema 25% = $\frac{1}{4}$

    $\frac{1}{4}$ of €20 = €_____

7. The following information was collected in the supermarket car park on Saturday. The pie chart shows how many of each colour car came into the car park that day.

    a) How many cars came into the car park altogether?

    b) What was the most popular colour in the car park that day?

    c) What was the least popular colour in the car park that day?

    d) What percentage of the cars were red?

    e) What percentage of the cars were yellow?

    f) Calculate the angle of each section of the pie chart. For example:

    Green = $\frac{10}{100}$ = $\frac{1}{10}$ and $\frac{1}{10}$ of 360° = _____

    Yellow = $\frac{15}{100}$ = $\frac{3}{20}$ and $\frac{3}{20}$ of 360° = _____

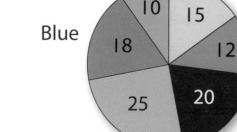

8. Draw a pie chart to represent the following data.

These children were asked to count how many letters were delivered to their house for a full week. Here are the results:

Michael: 10 letters
Brendan: 15 letters
Roísín: 20 letters
Amy: 15 letters

To find out how many degrees are in each section of the pie chart, we must find what fraction of the total number of letters was delivered to each person.

$$\text{So the total} = 10 + 15 + 20 + 15 = 60$$

Michael: $\frac{10}{60} = \frac{1}{6}$. To find the size of the angle for this on the pie chart, we find $\frac{1}{6}$ of 360° = _____.

When all of the angles have been calculated, draw a full circle and divide it up accordingly using your protractor.

Remember to label each fraction of your pie chart.

9. Mrs Walsh had €120 at the beginning of the week and spent the money on the following items. Represent her spending on a pie chart.

School books:	€15
Groceries:	€60
Clothes:	€30
Petrol:	€15

10. Represent these basketball results on a pie chart.

Player	Cian	John	Ciara	Andrew
Number of Points Scored	12	8	16	12

11. Carry out an investigation of the eye colour of 20 of your classmates. Draw a pie chart to display your results.

Data Sets

1. Your task is to collect a top-secret set of data on the vital statistics of your classmates. Collect the information under the following headings from as many people as possible.

Name	Age (Years, Months)	Hair Colour	Height (m, cm)	Shoe Size

If possible, record the data in a database program on a computer.

Now answer these questions on your set of data.

a) How many people in total have contributed to your data set?

b) Who is the oldest person recorded?

c) Who is the youngest person recorded?

d) What percentage of the people surveyed have brown hair?

e) Draw a pie chart to display the hair colour of the people surveyed.

f) What is the most popular shoe size? How many people surveyed have this shoe size?

g) Name the tallest and the smallest people surveyed.

h) What is the difference in height between the tallest person and smallest person?

i) Show the shoe sizes of you classmates on a bar chart.

2. Complete a study on the hair colour of 15 people. Draw a table to record your findings. Represent these findings using one of these charts: bar chart, multiple bar chart or pie chart.

   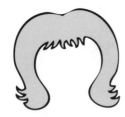

3. Organise a soccer / basketball / unihoc tournament. Make a table to record the results of the matches.

a) Which teams won, lost and drew the most matches?

b) Show the points on a pie chart.
   Remember to add up all the points to get your total.

Team	Won	Lost	Draw	Points

Homework

1. Construct a bar chart showing the favourite sport of those surveyed in the table below.

Favourite Sport	Hurling	Football	Basketball	Soccer	Hockey	Rugby
Number of People	16	18	12	20	10	14

2. Record the attendance information of the pupils in 5th class on a multiple bar chart.

Day	Monday	Tuesday	Wednesday	Thursday	Friday
Boys	13	15	14	13	12
Girls	14	15	17	16	15

3. This table shows the favourite fruit of 120 children. Can you work out from the pie chart how many children preferred each individual fruit?

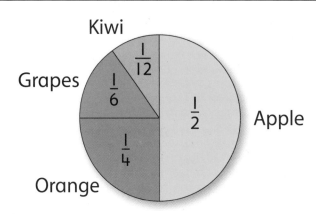

4. Construct a pie chart to represent what season a group of people's birthdays are in.

Season	Spring	Summer	Autumn	Winter
Number of People	18	3	6	9

Recap

- I can read and construct bar charts. ○ ○ ○
- I can read and construct multiple bar charts. ○ ○ ○
- I can interpret pie charts. ○ ○ ○
- I can construct pie charts. ○ ○ ○
- I can record data sets. ○ ○ ○

28. Area 1

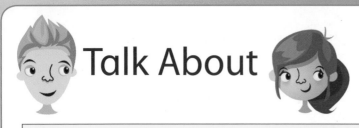 Talk About

Area is the amount of space contained within a 2-D shape.

The area is the coloured space inside the shape.

Shade in the area of this 'shape.'

But how do we measure the amount of space inside a shape? Can you measure space with a ruler? Try it.

To measure space, we need a unit of measurement that takes up space.

To avoid confusion, everyone uses the same units of measurement when working out area. We call these **standard units of measurement**.

The standard units used in measuring area are a square centimetre (cm^2) and a square metre (m^2).

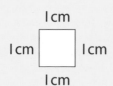

This is a square centimetre. As you can see, it's a square that has sides that are 1 cm in length.

What, do you think, is a square metre and why have we not drawn it on the page to show you?

Why do we need different standard units of measurement of area?

Strand: Measures
Curriculum Objectives:
Discover that the area of a rectangle is length by breadth; calculate area using square centimetres and square metres.

What is the area of a rectangle that is 4cm long and 2cm wide?

Each of the small squares has sides that are 1cm long, so they are square centimetres (cm²).

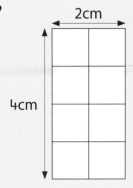

There are 4 rows of 2, so:

    Length = 4cm
    Width = 2cm
    Area = 8cm²

So to work out the area of shapes like tables and notice boards – **rectangles** – we just need to know the length and the width of the rectangle.

How would you write down a rule for working out the area of a rectangle if you know the length and the width of the rectangle?

If the length and the width are measured in cm, then your answer should be in cm².
If the length and the width are in m, then your answer should be in m².

---

1. Work out the areas of these rectangles.

    a) length 25cm
       width 16cm

    b) length 29cm
       width 18cm

    c) length 32m
       width 24m

    d) length 17m
       width 27m

    e) length 35cm
       width 31cm

    f) length 34m
       width 48m

2. Work out the areas of these squares.

    a) length 23cm

    b) length 39m

    c) length 14cm

    d) length 37cm

    e) length 19m

    f) length 43m

3. Draw rectangles of these dimensions into your copy and write their areas under them. You may decorate the rectangles if you wish. Remember: the squares in your copies are not square centimetres.

    a) **Rectangle 1**
       length 6cm
       width 3cm

    b) **Rectangle 2**
       length 4cm
       width 9cm

    c) **Rectangle 3**
       length 7cm
       width 2cm

    d) **Rectangle 4**
       length 12cm
       width 5cm

    e) **Rectangle 5**
       length 8cm
       width 7cm

    f) **Rectangle 6**
       length 9cm
       width 10cm

Homework

1. Measure the area of the following objects at home using your maths book.

   a) TV screen   b) kitchen table   c) your bed   d) a radiator

2. We use different sizes of envelope for different types of letter. Work out the area of these envelopes.

   a) length 13cm
      width 8cm

   b) length 12cm
      width 16cm

   c) length 18cm
      width 25cm

   d) length 27cm
      width 17cm

   e) length 33cm
      width 24cm

   f) length 38cm
      width 49cm

3. Draw the following rectangles into your copy and decorate them. Calculate their area.

   a) **Rectangle 1**
      length 7cm
      width 5cm

   b) **Rectangle 2**
      length 6cm
      width 6cm

   c) **Rectangle 3**
      length 4cm
      width 9cm

4. Draw the following squares into your copy and decorate them. Calculate their area.

   a) length 8cm   b) length 5cm   c) length 11cm

Recap

- I can use different objects to measure area.   ○ ○ ○

- I know what the rule is for measuring the area of rectangles.   ○ ○ ○

- I know why we use standard units of measurement.   ○ ○ ○

- I can calculate the area of rectangles.   ○ ○ ○

29. Capacity

Talk About

Instruments That Measure Capacity

Examine the following containers. Discuss which would hold more liquid and which would hold less liquid. How would you measure how much liquid each container holds?

Capacity is a measure of the amount of liquid a container can hold.

Units That Measure Capacity

1. Fill in the blanks using the words litre and millilitre.

   a) The most common unit of measuring capacity is the _____.

   b) Smaller quantities of liquid are measured using the _____.

2. Draw and label 5 liquids you can buy in containers that are measured in:

   a) litres   b) millilitres

3. Choose the correct capacity.

   a) Does a petrol can have a capacity of 5 millilitres or 5 litres?

   b) Does a cup have a capacity of 240 millilitres or 240 litres?

   c) Does a tablespoon have a capacity of 15 millilitres or 15 litres?

   d) Does a bucket have a capacity of 7 millilitres or 7 litres?

Strand: Measures
Curriculum Objectives:
Select and use appropriate instruments of measurement;
estimate and measure capacity using appropriate metric units.

4. In how many different capacity containers can you buy milk? List them in order, starting with the smallest.

Remember: 1000 millilitres (ml) = 1 litre (l)

$1\,ml = \frac{1}{1000}$ litre = 0.001 litre

5. How many millilitres?
   a) If there is $\frac{1}{2}$ litre of juice left in a carton, how many millilitres of juice are left?
   b) If I drank $\frac{1}{4}$ litre of lemonade, how many millilitres of lemonade did I drink?
   c) A jug has a capacity of $\frac{3}{4}$ litres. How many millilitres does it hold?

6. Put these containers in order, starting with the container that holds the least amount of liquid.

7. Fill in the blanks in this table.

ml	l ml	l
1345ml		
	4l 271ml	
		3.506l
	1l 2ml	
		3.92l
5065ml		
	2l 305ml	
		2.4l
6700ml		

8. a) Collect a jar and a small bucket. Estimate how many jars of water it would take to fill the bucket.
   b) Measure how many jars it takes by pouring filled jars into the bucket. Record your results.
   c) Using a graduated jug, measure the capacity of the jar. Then find the capacity of the bucket.

9. How much liquid is in each graduated jug?

a)   b)   c)   d)   e)

10. a) Would you use a graduated jug or a litre container to measure the capacity of each of these?

   b) Collect each of the above containers and measure how much water each can hold using the appropriate instrument.

11. Estimate and then measure the capacity of each of the following classroom containers using the appropriate instrument of measurement.
   a) paint holder   b) lunchbox   c) beaker   d) jar

12. Can you write these capacities as millilitres?
   a) 1 litre 249ml   b) 2 litres 692ml   c) 4 litres 80ml
   d) 3 litres 5ml   e) 4 litres 75ml   f) 1.5 litres
   g) 2.6 litres   h) 3.15 litres   i) 9.08 litres

13. a) Collect a variety of objects in the classroom that can hold water and estimate their capacities.
   b) Measure and record these capacities.
   c) List them in order, starting with the greatest capacity.

14. Match the capacity.
   a) Glass   40 litres
   b) Washing machine   5ml
   c) Bath   10 litres
   d) Bottle of wine   750ml
   e) Fish tank   200 litres
   f) Small spoon   250ml

15. Would you use litres or millilitres to measure each of the following containers?
   a) watering can   b) medicine bottle   c) yoghurt carton   d) sink
   e) soup ladle   f) wine glass   g) wheelie bin   h) pond

Adding Capacity

Jenny is having a party and has bought 6 litres of lemonade. She needs to find out if the 2 jugs she has will be enough to hold all 6 litres. The capacities of the jugs are 3585ml and 2 litres 705ml. Add them to see if they will hold the 6 litres.

Adding capacities can be done in 3 different ways:

a)
```
    3585ml
  + 2705ml
  _____
```

b)
litres	millilitres
3	585
+ 2	705

c)
```
    litres
    3.585
  + 2.705
  _____
```

Add each of the sums to see if you get the same answer.

1. Now try these. Remember to change them to the same units before you start.
   a) 2098ml + 3l 504ml + 1.3l
   b) 4.12l + 345ml + 2l 35ml
   c) 5.798l + 2l 3ml + 1056ml
   d) 9.456l + 1067ml + 4l 7ml
   e) 127ml + 3l 120ml + 2.9l
   f) 1l 65ml + 4.1l + 3905ml

Subtracting Capacity

2. Now try these subtraction questions. Remember to change capacities to the same unit first.
   a) 4650ml – 1.25l
   b) 2l 450ml – 1987ml
   c) 3.45l – 768ml
   d) 3090ml – 2l 680ml
   e) 6l 20ml – 4.378l
   f) 4.5l – 3l 120ml

3. Complete the following.
   a) 500ml = _____ litre
   b) 0.6 litres = _____ ml
   c) $\frac{1}{4}$ litre = _____ml
   d) 3.504 litres _____ml
   e) 12l 627ml = _____ litres
   f) $\frac{2}{5}$ litre = _____ml
   g) 4008ml = _____ litres
   h) 0.045 litres = _____ml

4. Use your calculator for the following. (Hint: convert all capacities to the same unit first.)

    a) 68l 450ml + 40l 35ml – 15l 780ml

    b) 103.5l + 56l 200ml – 78.9l

    c) 2058ml + 4l 389ml – 1.7l

    d) 156l 550ml – (26.670l + 114l 4ml)

Multiplying Capacity

Nigel is going to paint his large shed and will need about 20 litres of paint. If 1 tin of paint has a capacity of 2.658 litres, what is the capacity of 8 tins?

a)
	ml
	2658
×	8

b)
	l	ml
	2	658
×		8

c)
	l
	2.658
×	8

Do you get the same answer for each different way of doing it?

If he bought 8 tins, how much paint will Nigel have left over after using his 20 litres?

5. Have a go at these.

    a) 4.590l × 5

    b) 6l 45ml × 3

    c) 13.5l × 7

    d) 1298ml × 9

    e) 5.78l × 4

    f) 9065ml × 6

    g) 7.65l × 12

    h) 4l 800ml × 25

    i) 8072ml × 19

6. For the class party, the teacher needs to fill 30 glasses of orange, each with a capacity of 250ml. How many litre bottles of orange will she need?

7. What is the total capacity of 5 oil tanks if each holds 45l 250ml?

8. A car uses 1 litre of petrol every 14km. How far would the car go on 25.5 litres of petrol?

Dividing Capacity

If Jim's family used 8l 250ml of milk over 5 days, on average how much milk did they use each day?

		l	ml	
a) 5$\overline{|8250}$ml	b) 5$\overline{|8\quad250}$			c) 5$\overline{|8.250}$ litres

Do you get the same answer for each different way of doing it?

9. Now try these.
   a) 3.568l ÷ 4
   b) 9l 350ml ÷ 5
   c) 4674ml ÷ 6
   d) 12l 40ml ÷ 8
   e) 66.95l ÷ 10
   f) 8l 750ml ÷ 7
   g) 22.368l ÷ 12
   h) 35l 400ml ÷ 15
   i) 42.575l ÷ 25

10. Ciara has a cough and her mother bought her a 100ml bottle of cough medicine. If Ciara has to take a 5ml spoon of cough medicine twice a day, how many days will the cough medicine last?

11. A glass holds $\frac{1}{4}$ litre. How many glasses can be filled from a barrel containing 16.25 litres?

Homework

1. Find 10 containers in your kitchen at home that are measured using litres or millilitres. Record them in a table.
    a) Which item has the largest capacity?
    b) Which item has the smallest capacity?
    c) What is the total capacity of the containers?

2. Can you write these as litres and millilitres?
    a) 4098ml
    b) 2.675l
    c) 1090ml
    d) 3.86l
    e) 7632ml
    f) 2.4l
    g) 5005ml
    h) 7.034l
    i) 97ml

3. Can you write these capacities as millilitres?
    a) 1l 637ml
    b) 2l 9ml
    c) 7l 430ml
    d) 8l 8ml
    e) 4.916l
    f) 1.85l
    g) 3.9l
    h) 0.085l
    i) 7.332l

4. Can you write these capacities as litres using the decimal point?

   a) 1l 163ml

   b) 2470ml

   c) 3l 7ml

   d) 8l 95ml

   e) 367ml

   f) 5ml

5. Now try these. Remember to change them to the same units before you start.

   a) 7l 32ml + 1.95l + 685ml

   b) 2098ml + 4l 708ml + 6.09l

   c) 8.376l + 5520ml + 6l 198ml

   d) 6.9l + 59ml + 5l 9ml

   e) 9035ml + 7l 450ml + 3.62l

   f) 4l 93ml + 0.635l + 5739ml

6. a) 5l 25ml – 1.76l

   b) 9004ml – 5.36l

   c) 2.816l – 1l 798ml

   d) 8l 127ml – 3693ml

   e) 6025ml – 4.167l

   f) 10.1l – 6l 249ml

7. Have a go at these.

   a) 7145ml × 8

   b) 2.809l × 9

   c) 8l 84ml × 7

   d) 2.083l × 15

   e) 5l 369ml × 27

   f) 3194ml × 34

8. Now try these.

   a) 2032ml ÷ 8

   b) 5l 892ml ÷ 4

   c) 3.174l ÷ 6

   d) 13.44l ÷ 14

   e) 1206ml ÷ 18

   f) 1l 8ml ÷ 24

Recap

- I know what instruments to use when measuring capacity. ◯ ◯ ◯

- I know the most appropriate unit of measurement to use. ◯ ◯ ◯

- I can add capacities. ◯ ◯ ◯

- I can subtract capacities. ◯ ◯ ◯

- I can multiply capacities. ◯ ◯ ◯

- I can divide capacities. ◯ ◯ ◯

30. Averages

Talk About

What Are Averages?

Meet Average Joe. Joe is 177cm tall. He weighs 78kg.
He has 100000 hairs on his head and can expect to live until
he is 78 years old.

These statistics are based on the averages for Irish men.
So if Jack is 83 years of age, 169cm tall and 81 kg in weight,
what can we say about him?

What would be the similar statistics for Average Jane?

Calculate Averages

Here is a chart of the class's attendance for last week.

Monday	Tuesday	Wednesday	Thursday	Friday
28	32	30	26	29

Calculate the average daily attendance.

Add the numbers: $28 + 32 + 30 + 26 + 29 = 145$

Then divide by the number of days: $145 \div 5 = 29$

Strand: Data
Curriculum Objectives:
Explore and calculate averages of simple data sets;
use data sets to solve problems.

1. a) On which day was the attendance exactly average?

    b) On how many days was it below average?

    c) On how many days was it above average?

2. Find the average of each of these. Estimate your answer first.

    a) 12, 15, 13, 17, 18   b) 56c, 26c, 40c, 62c   c) 78g, 69g, 90g, 85g, 83g

    d) 4.1, 5.3, 6.8, 5.2, 3.6   e) 10cm, 16cm, 14cm, 12cm   f) 9, 23, 13, 18, 22

    g) 1358, 1560, 1432   h) 110km, 99km, 111km, 88km   i) 5, 6, 9, 3, 8, 4, 7

3. Jenny read 48 pages of her book on Monday, 36 pages on
    Tuesday and 72 pages on Wednesday. What was the average
    number of pages she read over the 3 days?

4. Have a look at these weather measurements for last week.

Day of the Week	Midday Temperature	Hours of Sunshine
Monday	16°C	5
Tuesday	15°C	6
Wednesday	18°C	4
Thursday	16°C	6
Friday	19°C	8
Saturday	22°C	10
Sunday	20°C	10

a) What were the highest and the lowest temperatures reached last week?

b) Find the difference between these 2 temperatures.

c) What 2 days had the same temperature recorded last week?

d) What was the average temperature last
    week?

e) What days had the greatest number of
    hours of sunshine last week?

f) Name the day that had half the number of
    hours of sunshine of other days.

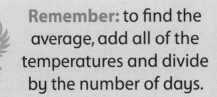

Remember: to find the
average, add all of the
temperatures and divide
by the number of days.

g) What was the average number of hours of sunshine for Wednesday and
    Thursday?

h) Find the average number of hours of sunshine for last week.

5. This bar chart shows the distance each person cycled in 1 day.
   a) From the chart, find the most frequent distance cycled.
   b) Calculate the average distance cycled.
   c) Did 1 of the cyclists cycle exactly the average distance?
   d) Name the cyclists who cycled below the average distance.
   e) Name the cyclists who cycled above the average distance.

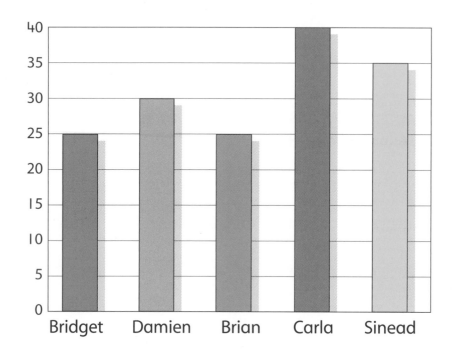

Puzzler

James has done 4 maths tests during the course of the year so far. His average score for the 4 tests is 78%. There are still 3 tests left in the year and James hopes to push his average score up to 90%. Is this possible?

6. Write down the ages of all of the children in your family and calculate the average. Also find the average height, weight and shoe size of the children.

7. If a car had driven 18000km after 1 year, can you work out the average monthly kilometres travelled?

8. Find the average goals scored by each of these teams.

Team	Dublin City	Wexford Wanderers	Roscommon Rovers
Goals Scored	2, 3, 2, 5, 2, 4	1, 1, 0, 0, 2, 0, 3, 1	2, 4, 2, 1, 1, 3, 1

9. Use your calculator to help you with these questions.

Airline	No. of Passengers	Price of Fare
Atlantic Air	335	€99.00
Fast-Jet	280	€125.00
Sky	310	€140.00
Go-Fly	175	€110.00

a) How many people travelled on the 4 airlines?

b) Find the average passenger load.

c) Find the average fare.

d) On which airlines were the passengers paying above average fare?

e) Calculate how much each airline collected in fares.

f) Calculate the average amount collected between the 4 airlines.

Puzzler

The average of 4 numbers is 85. Find the fourth number if 3 of the numbers are 92, 74 and 81.

Homework

1. Find the average of each of these number sets. Estimate your answer first.

   a) 21, 18, 20, 24, 17

   b) 98cm, 104cm, 101cm

   c) €1.45, €1.64, €1.58, €1.37

   d) 53m, 75m, 43m

   e) 1.9, 2.4, 3.5, 2.6

   f) 78, 43, 81, 64, 99

2. The following shows the number of packets of biscuits sold in a shop over the course of the week.

   a) What is the average number of packets of biscuits sold over the 5 days?

   b) How many days were sales above average and how many days were they below average?

   c) If 35 packets were sold on Saturday and 27 packets were sold on Sunday, how would that change the average number sold over the whole week?

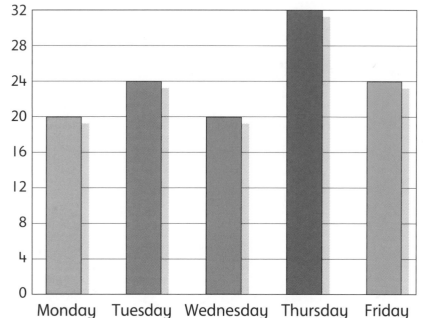

Film	Attendance in 1st Week	Box Office Receipts
The Midas Touch	3965	€29980
Justice Is Served	1259	€9560
You Can't Hurry Love	4741	€34200
A Summer of Solitude	823	€6140

3. a) What was the average attendance at the 4 films?

   b) What were the average takings?

Recap

- I know what averages are.   ○ ○ ○

- I know how to calculate the average of a set of numbers.   ○ ○ ○

31. Area 2

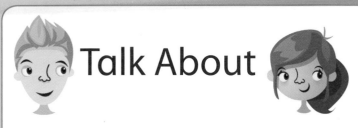

Talk About

Area of Rectangles

1. Estimate the areas of the following rectangles. (Hint: estimate the length and the width first.)

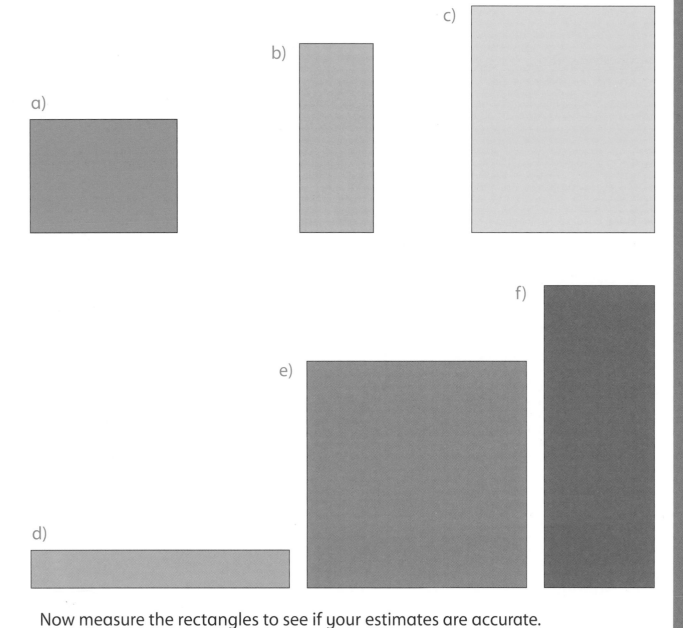

Now measure the rectangles to see if your estimates are accurate.

Strand: Measures
Curriculum Objectives:
Estimate and measure the area of regular and irregular 2-D shapes;
calculate area using square centimetres and square metres.

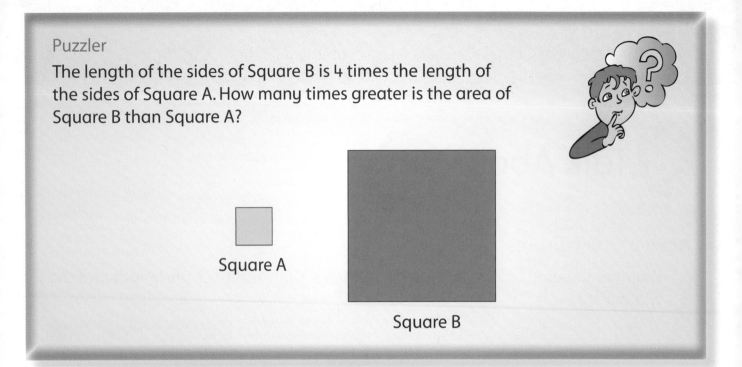

Puzzler

The length of the sides of Square B is 4 times the length of the sides of Square A. How many times greater is the area of Square B than Square A?

Square A

Square B

Units of Measurement

1. Out in the yard, use a piece of chalk to draw a square centimetre and a square metre beside it (use a metre stick).

   a) Can you work out how many cm² would fit into 1 m²?

   b) List 5 things whose area would be measured in cm².

   c) List 5 things whose area would be measured in m².

2. a) Estimate the areas of these objects. Use the most appropriate unit.

   b) Measure the objects afterwards to see how close your estimates are.

   c) What instruments would you use to measure these objects?

Object	Unit Used	Estimate of Area	Actual Area
Maths book			
Classroom			
Maths copy			
Whiteboard			
Art paper			
School yard			

Calculate Missing Dimensions

1. Estimate the areas of these shapes. (Hint: estimate as if they were complete rectangles first and then estimate the piece(s) that is missing.)

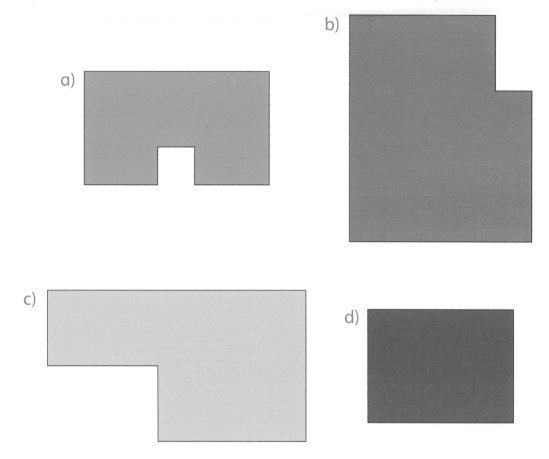

a)

b)

c)

d)

If a bookmark has an area of 72cm² and is 4cm wide, how long is the bookmark?

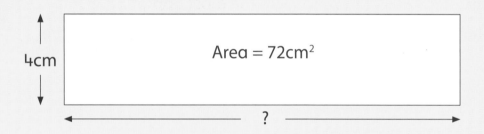

4cm

Area = 72cm²

?

We know that **area = length × width**.

So 72 = ? × 4

and   4 ⌜72
          18cm

2. Work out the missing dimension of these photographs.

a) area 153cm²
length 9cm

b) area 182m²
length 7m

c) area 324 cm²
length 12cm

d) area 312m²
width 8m

e) area 240cm²
width 16cm

f) area 432m²
width 24m

3. Now fill in the missing measurements of these gardens.

Garden	Length	Width	Area
1	34m	27m	
2		11m	198m²
3	6m		108m²
4	19m	28m	
5		13m	338m²
6	46m	75m	
7	26m		936m²

4. John's family moved to a new house. Because he is the eldest, he can choose which bedroom he would like for himself. He wants to choose the bigger of the 2 bedrooms, but he is not sure which one is in fact bigger.
Can you help him choose?

Bedroom 1:   2.8m × 3m
Bedroom 2:   2m × 3.9m

Bedroom 1   Bedroom 2

What is the difference in area between the 2 bedrooms?

5. John's sister, Ciara, has been given the bedroom that John didn't want. She is choosing a new carpet for her room but she has been told that it cannot cost any more than €200. The type of carpet she has chosen costs €26 per square metre. Does she have enough money?

6. a) John's father laid a patio in the new house. He used square paving slabs that are 48cm long. What is the area of each of the paving slabs?

b) If the area of the patio is 28.5m² and the patio is 5m wide, how long is it?

7. The perimeter of the garden is 46m and the width of the garden is 9m. What is the area of the garden?

Homework

1. Estimate and measure the areas of these rectangles.

a)

b)

c)

d)

e)

2. Fill in the following table.

Object	Unit Used	Estimate of Area	Actual Area
TV screen			
Bed			
Bedroom floor			
Kitchen table			
Back garden			

3. Estimate and measure the areas of the following shapes.

a)

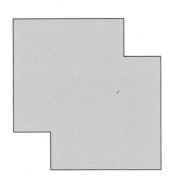

b)

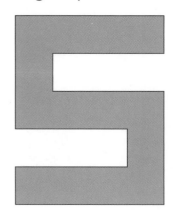

4. Fill in the missing measurements of these books.

Book	Length	Width	Area
1	25cm		400cm²
2	29cm	18cm	
3		23cm	437cm²
4	35cm	26cm	
5		37cm	999cm²
6	34cm		714cm²
7	28cm	36cm	

Recap

- I can estimate and measure the areas of rectangles.

- I know the most appropriate unit of measurement to use.

- I can calculate missing dimensions.